A LIFETIME WITH 'O' GAUGE
CREWCHESTER — AND OTHERS

JACK RAY

A PENDRAGON BOOK FROM ATLANTIC TRANSPORT PUBLISHERS

Frontispiece illustration:
The author with a group of young Crewchester Model Railway
Club members. August 1977.

Front cover:
''Royal'' Claud Hamilton 4-4-0 No. 8787 approaches
Crewchester Junction with an up semi-fast train.

Back cover:
Class 5 leaves Ravensmoor terminus with an LMS express
for the south.

To Dave Rowlands
whose benevolent bullying and kindly encouragement sustained
me during its writing.

© Jack L. Ray and Atlantic Transport Publishers 1992

'Pendragon Books' is an imprint of Atlantic Transport Publishers,
'Trevithick House', West End, Penryn, Cornwall TR10 8HE
All rights reserved.

Set in Berling by Royd Typesetting, Keighley, West Yorkshire.

Layout and Design by Barry C. Lane.

Colour and Black and White photographic reproduction by
The Amadeus Press Ltd, Huddersfield, West Yorkshire.

All photographs by the Author unless otherwise credited.
Thanks are due to the East Anglian Daily Times Newspapers Ltd.
for permission to use photographs taken by them of the
Crewchester Model Railway.

British Cataloguing in Publication Data.
A catalogue record for this book is available from the British Library.

ISBN 0 906899 54 0

CONTENTS

PUBLISHER'S INTRODUCTION

I have known Jack Ray personally for a relatively short time, but it is a measure of his appeal and importance to the model railway fraternity that I feel I have known him for more than half a life-time, for is he not one of those few people whose overall influence in the hobby seems to well exceed the sum total of any of the individual contributions which he may have made? I make this point in the full realisation that it will cause him acute embarrass-ment(!), not least because his 'style' (there is no other word which I can immediately call to mind) is such that it has instant appeal to all modellers, never mind whether or not they agree with his ideas or follow his standards or example – as a matter of fact, most of us don't, for a whole variety of reasons and probably to our detriment!

Jack has been active in the model railway field for more years than I care to recall, during which time his efforts have proved an inspiration to hundreds if not thousands of railway modellers. He has written articles in most of the model journals (past and present) regarding his trials and tribulations and, as its first President and Chairman, was one of the small band of enthusiasts who were instrumental in ensuring that the fledgling Gauge 'O' Guild managed safely to leave the nest in the 1950s! Without this impetus, 7mm scale modelling in Britain could well have 'died on its feet' a generation or more ago. If for nothing else, those of us who espouse this superb modelling scale would have ample reason to be grateful. But on top of this, Jack had a demanding career before his retirement in 1980 – and as if that was not enough, much of his spare time was occupied in unremitting, tireless and totally unpaid efforts on behalf of many generations of youngsters. Such a man can only command our respect.

The linking theme was always railways and although Jack claims to be just an ordinary fellow with a deep love of the subject and possessed of no great modelling skills, he probably undersells himself. But it is this characteristic which explains why so many other folk can and do relate to him so well – he is in all vital senses a 'fellow spirit' and although I am one of many who follow a different road in my own modelling activities, he has always commanded my great admiration and I am proud that he should have let me write this introduction.

In this quite enchanting review of his life in the hobby, Jack has written a delightful combination of autobiography and modelling reminiscence. In it he tells of his own experiences and of the many people he has met during a long modelling life; not a few of them are now legendary in the hobby. It is a modest, self-depreciating account, yet it is also inspirational in the sense that Jack bears no sense of envy towards those whose skills exceed his own. But what he perhaps does not realise (which, of course, is what makes it especially appealing) is that his extraordinary capacity to 'turn an apposite phrase' and make his observations both readable and relevant, is just as important in the promotion of the hobby to a wider field as is any unique dexterity on the lathe or workbench!

In my working life as a publisher I am obliged to read many manuscripts, some of which are very difficult going indeed. Yet, as a writer myself, I am also conscious of how hard it is to get the right word in context yet simultaneously keep the attention of the reader – and none of us are perfect anyway; so it was with a real sense of undiluted joy that I read Jack's first draft when he sent it to me, for I could not put it down – and that was a rare experience indeed. It read like a good novel and I was therefore delighted when he asked me if I would like to consider publishing it.

If and when a definitive history of this fascinating hobby is ever written, I don't suppose that Jack Ray's name will figure prominently amongst those who made a significant contribution to its technical progress – I suspect he would not want it so and be simultaneously both amazed and embarrassed to think of it in such terms! But if we consider the subject in the broader sense in terms of encouraging the ordinary man to 'have a go', no matter how many 'left thumbs' he may have (to quote one of Jack's favourite phrases), then this man's lifetime dedication, good humour and underlying modesty has lessons for us all and will live for all time. As such I commend his story to you, for it is an optimistic account by a very happy man of his life and experiences – and it will certainly make you laugh. It may also make you cry at times; but that is its strength and I am delighted to be involved with it.

David Jenkinson

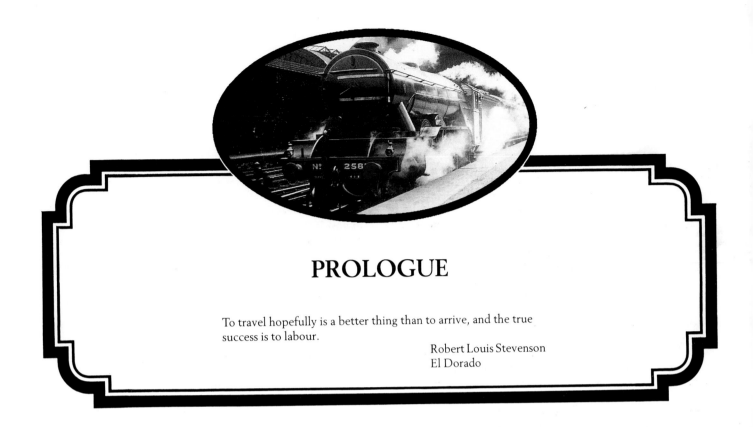

PROLOGUE

To travel hopefully is a better thing than to arrive, and the true success is to labour.

Robert Louis Stevenson
El Dorado

In 1916 the Battles of Verdun, Jutland, and the Somme were fought, daylight-saving was introduced, and all-out submarine warfare commenced in earnest. Against such a background of world-shattering upheavals there occured in the sequestered Essex village of Dedham an event of monumental insignificance – save to my parents and myself – for on 27th December I was set gingerly upon life's permanent way. The union of a cost-accountant and a school teacher hardly suggested the emergence of a budding Beeson or a promising Bassett-Lowke, and indeed I seemed to have been born with five thumbs on each hand, so there would appear to be no logical reason for my almost instant and obsessive fascination by railways in general and steam engines in particular. The close proximity of the Great Northern branch from Finsbury Park certainly accounts for my early awareness of steam trains, for the line passed within sight and sound of our home in north London. Removal in 1921 to Hendon where our house backed on to the six-track Midland Railway main line between Brent sidings and Hendon station offered a rich diet for the embryonic train-enthusiast, and so it was my young brother and I were spiritually nourished by the gospels of Johnson, Deeley, Fowler, and others until well into our teens.

From 1921 to 1932 I was offered my education, firstly at a kindergarten, followed by three years in a so-called council-school, from which I graduated to the William Ellis School in Highgate, where in 1932, during the great Depression, when my father suffered two 5% cuts in his meagre salary, I was deemed to have wasted enough of the family exchequer in Highgate, and, with a younger brother to educate, was launched upon the world of business and industry in the capacity of office boy. My time at the William Ellis school had not, however, been entirely wasted, for in 1927 I became the delighted owner of a season ticket between Hendon and Kentish Town on the old Midland (but by now LMS) line. Even though the Grouping of the railway companies had taken place four years previously, we were still known as the "Midland boys", a nomenclature which earned us the privileges of missing Prayers in the morning, and, in the event of us suffering Detention after school, permitted us to be released fifteen minutes before full time; all this by reason of train timings. One of my compatriots on the railway was Geoffrey Sparkes whose father was an executive on the railway, thereby gaining us much inside information on railway matters and turning us into a bunch of know-all authorities at school, where, naturally, anything pertaining to trains was of primary interest to almost everyone.

There was another important factor in this period relevant to my development as a railway enthusiast. My season ticket took me to within a 3d return fare of St. Pancras, so on a half holiday or Saturday I would squander my weekly pocket money (3d), travel to St. Pancras, and cross the road there to King's Cross station where my greatest allegiance lay – the Great Northern – land of Gresley, Ivatt, et al, where trains of beautiful varnished teak, headed by Gresley's superb Pacifics came and went. Three-pence, old money, has its nearest equivalent in today's money of round about one penny, and very few of my peers ever had more than this as weekly pocket money. One old penny would buy a box of matches, take one a mile or more on bus or tram, buy a bar of chocolate, or two large sticky buns at the school tuck-shop. To a teen-aged boy who had expended that entire sum on the rail fare, to walk along platform 10 at King's Cross, peering into the opulent pink-shaded luxury of the Pullman trains was to gaze upon a different world, inhabited by only the very wealthy. Even to this day, when seated beside the Crewchester line at a terminus and watching the tender of an LNER Pacific setting back on to a train of

1

teak stock, my mind flies back to those days in the 1930s and platform 10, King's Cross, seeing those magnificent monsters backing out of Gasworks tunnel.

Like most of my generation, I owned a Hornby tinplate train set, comprising an 0-4-0 nondescript tender-engine, an open wagon, a petrol tanker and brake-van, to which basic stock I gradually added points and further rails. Next door lived the Town Clerk of Hendon, whose financial status allowed him to equip his son – a lad of my own age – with Bassett Lowke trains. Our mutual personal dislike and frequent fights precluded me from sharing these fine models, but I could observe over the fence during rare intervals of armed truce, and watch his 4-4-0 haul bogie-Pullman coaches over a complex system laid out over the patio. And then in 1930, I think it was, two of my 'Midland' boy friends and I visited the Schoolboys' Exhibition at Olympia. Here, for the first time in my life I saw a model railway – as distinct from tinplate track laid out on a table or floor. The rails were correct bullhead, the points were of the pattern of their prototype – not tinplate sectors pivoting on a bifurcated rivet – and the lines ran through cuttings, tunnels, and detailed miniature stations. Recognisable models of familiar engines such as Midland compounds headed trains of crimson bogie stock: Fowler 0-6-0s passed with trains of private-owner wagons, and indeed I beheld a microcosm of the world I knew. It was to me as if I had seen the Holy Grail, so dramatic was the impact of that model railway, and inch by inch I fought my way to the barrier rail where, with bursting heart and bladder I remained, despite the constant pleas from my companions "Come ON, Ray – there's a lot more to see." Blind and deaf to their cries, I spent the remainder of that afternoon, devouring every tiny detail of what to me was perfection. To own such a system must surely be the peak of man's achievement! I am certain now that that one event generated the determination to own such a railway – one day!

It was also at this time, much to my shame, I must confess to 'borrowing' money from my mother's purse, often left within my reach, in order to take a 2d tram to Willesden or Neasden stations and buying a return ticket to Baker Street, there to see those curious Metropolitan express electric locomotives which worked trains out to Rickmansworth, there to be exchanged for steam engines on to Aylesbury. At Willesden Green I would spend much time watching the fine Great Central expresses pass on their own tracks, hauled by Robinson's beautiful 'Directors' and even more beautiful Atlantics, with their trains of distinctive 'Barnum' coaches. Such petty pilfering from Mother's purse was inevitably discovered and painful retribution would follow. These criminal propensities were in later life sublimated by the necessity to complete expense accounts to my firm.

From office-boy I graduated, purely on the strength of very amateur accomplishments on piano and church organ, to become the representative of a London music publisher, thereby casting off the shackles of office life in favour of long train journeys to every town and city in the British Isles, all 'on expenses'. Before the true motivation for my taking on this wonderful itinerant job became evident in falling sales figures, the War came along, and I spent six years in khaki, various postings and journeys on leave offering many fascinating train journeys. Upon demobilisation I took up the threads of civilian life by entering the firm of Novello's, the music publishers, and after marrying in 1949 I at last had my own house and garden where the long dormant desire to build a model railway was further encouraged by the acquisition of a step-son. With the lad's best interests at heart, I persuaded him to spend a £10 gift from a God-parent on a Bassett-Lowke compound and some steel track parts. With no adequate room indoors, perforce we took to the garden, and thus was Crewchester born.

EARLY DAYS

Most normal people, before starting on a project such as building a model railway, will sit down, think long and hard, read every available book and article on the subject relevant to their aims, and then draw up careful plans. My own approach differed from the norm in that I just jumped in, if not at the deep end, at least up to my neck in largely uncharted waters. The often highly unscientific blundering progress from one layout to the next has continued, more or less, for some forty years now, the various layouts being chronicled in great detail in a number of magazines, so it is not as a technical account of Crewchester in all its phases that this book is written; rather is it an autobiographical story telling of the developments and metamorphoses of Crewchester, with some emphasis upon the many people who have influenced my progress.

One principal aim throughout the entire history of the line has been to re-create in miniature – however crudely – the scenes I knew and loved in the age of steam; a desire which has intensified over the years as the steam engines disappeared, or have been relegated to "preserved" lines, and the railways savagely truncated, with the once-beautiful stations left lying about without decent burial, like rotting carcasses for all who pass to see.

In 1949 I married, inherited a step-son, and bought my first house in Kelvedon, Essex. During school term time my work took me away from home from Monday to Friday, but I did, to some extent, enjoy far more annual holiday than most people did at that time, when the norm was one fortnight per year, for my work in schools and colleges did allow me to take my holidays with those establishments, although various courses and conferences did take up quite a proportion of such leave. It is extremely hard now to appreciate fully the conditions which existed in relation to model railways. The War was over and people were concentrating their lives on picking up the threads of civilian life rather than indulging in hobbies. Food, clothing, and petrol were still rationed, and while these imposed hardship, especially as to travel, compared with the horrors of the six years we had just lived through, these things were little more than minor irritations.

At that time I was not even aware that there existed such publications as model railway magazines, so, with a small lad to bring up, I tended to encourage him in the medium with which I had grown up – Gauge 0 tinplate Hornby trains – and already these items were beginning to reappear in shops. My travels all over Britain gave me the inestimable advantage of getting to know shops in every city and town, some of them High Street toy shops; others little back-street bric-a-brac shops where one could find all manner of pre-war model railway items at give-away prices. Cash was scarce and there was little to spare for model railways, but it may be worth recalling some of the prices of those days. One could buy a brand-new Bassett-Lowke LMS compound for £7.75, or a *Flying Scotsman* in tinplate for £12. A Bassett-Lowke *Duchess of Montrose* was priced at just over £27, while the Stanier taper-

Before Crewchester. The very first garden layout at Kelvedon, showing the terminus named Rockhill.

boilered *Royal Scot* was marked £25.50. But in the second-hand shops one could pick up Exley coaches for between £1.50 and £1.75 each, complete with cast-iron Mansell wheels!

Fine and coarse scale were words I had never encountered, and would not have understood, for I was far too excited by the discovery of steel bullhead rail section, and points which were built on the same principle as the real thing. My visits to junk-shops resulted in two curious looking engines, built by Hornby in pre-war days, both of them 4-4-2 tender-engines, one bearing the name of *Flying Scotsman* and the other *Royal Scot*, later to be joined by yet a third, this time purporting to be a French engine, complete with two domes, and bogie-tender, painted in SCNF livery and labelled NORD. These locomotives were fitted with the fine 4-coupled Hornby No. 2 'special' clockwork mechanism, would run for some 100 feet and haul up to three cars with ease. It was the arrival of these big engines which brought about the decision to go out into the garden, for our rabbit-hutch of a house could no longer cope with the ambitious layouts of tinplate track, and the new bullhead rails demanded far more room.

At this point I became aware of the model railway magazines and began to take them regularly – the *Model Railway News*, the *Railway Modeller*, and the *Model Railway Constructor*. From these I heard of the Easter exhibition at Central Hall, Westminster, and started attending this important annual function. Certain names were beginning to become familiar through reading the magazines; Norman Eagles, P. D. Hancock, Geoff Bigmore (to name but three), and it was at Central Hall I was able to put faces to the names, and even meet some of them. The name

Crewchester had not yet been coined, and the railway in the garden comprised a crude length of steel track, with sleepers at 5in intervals, running down the side of the lawn from an equally crude terminus near the house to the lower half of the garden where it split at a junction, the main line going on to a four-platform covered terminus named Rockhill. From the junction, a double track loop ran round to yet another terminus. Of this layout the less said the better, for it lasted no more than a year, yet it was during that year (1951) that two people became involved with the hobby, Johnny Watts and John Blair.

Johnny Watts was a neighbour who, seeing this railway in the garden, showed interest, and quickly became a regular operator. The total stud was the brand-new Bassett-Lowke compound, the three Hornby 4-4-2 engines, and another Bassett-Lowke free-lance 4-4-0 bearing the exalted name of *Princess Elizabeth*, all of which managed a motley assortment of coaches, varying from Hornby Metropolitan bogies to the odd Exley coach and two early tinplate Bassett-Lowke LMS bogie cars. John Blair, on the other hand, lived a hundred miles away in Hertfordshire, and at one time we had shared lodgings in Potters Bar where we discovered mutual interests in railways and music, which led to an invitation to visit Kelvedon. John became a periodic visitor and for a number of years and was something of a partner in the venture.

In 1952, we decided to attempt something a little more ambitious, comprising a continuous circuit with one important station; a system which would be capable of operation by one person if necessary. As most of my stock was LMS, I sought a name for the station which evoke LMS territory, hence the fusion of two famous names, Crewe and Chester. Later, when LNER locomotives and stock appeared on the scene the name became somewhat irrelevant, but it stuck. Johnny Watts, seeing drawings by P.D. Hancock in a magazine, offered to build station buildings from these, and so the first Crewchester station was born, modelled unwittingly on Polton station NBR. The steel track caused us much trouble for, although it was sheridized, it soon rusted, and had to be scoured with coarse emery cloth before each running session. It was this layout which inspired me to offer the very first article to the *Railway Modeller* whose editor, to my surprise, published it in the November 1953 issue.

In 1953, however, we moved house to Ipswich, bidding farewell to Johnny Watts, and re-naming the free-lance 4-4-0 after him. That engine deserves further mention, for it lay in a direct line of models produced by Bassett-Lowke for B.D.V.* Cigarette coupon gifts, the first one being another 4-4-0 named *Duke of York*. It is interesting to reflect that when the contract was made between

Bassett-Lowke and B.D.V., the production cost of the engine was not to exceed ten shillings (50p). Bassett-Lowke in fact lost money on that production run, but were able to recoup their losses by the sales which followed. Two of these 'Duke of York' engines eventually found their way on to Crewchester metals. After the *Duke of York* came a different model, still a 4-4-0 but this time with a continuous splasher over the drivers, the aforementioned *Princess Elizabeth*. Finally in line of succession came yet another post-war version, very similar to *Princess Elizabeth*, but this time named *Prince Charles*.

The publication of the article on the Kelvedon layout led to many letters from readers, and gained me an introduction to Norman Eagles, veteran of 'The Sherwood Section of the LMS', quite the best-known clockwork operated railway in Britain. We met at one of the Easter exhibitions at Central Hall where Norman introduced me to Geoff Bigmore, whose Bigston Line I had read about in the press. It was here that I first encountered a man who, to many of us, was almost a demi-god, J.N. Maskelyne, AILocoE, Editor of the *Model Railway News*. My first meeting with this great man was brief in the extreme, but we did discover that his office lay close to the head office of my own firm in Soho, and he invited me to drop in for a chat whenever I happened to be in town.

* – *a popular brand of cigarette and tobacco in pre 1939-war days, the initials standing (so I am told) for 'BEST DARK VIRGINIA'.*

The first Crewchester station, built by Johnny Watts, from drawings by P.D. Hancock of Poulton NBR station. The engine is a Bassett-Lowke compound and the coaches a mixture of ancient Exley and home-made cardboard stock.

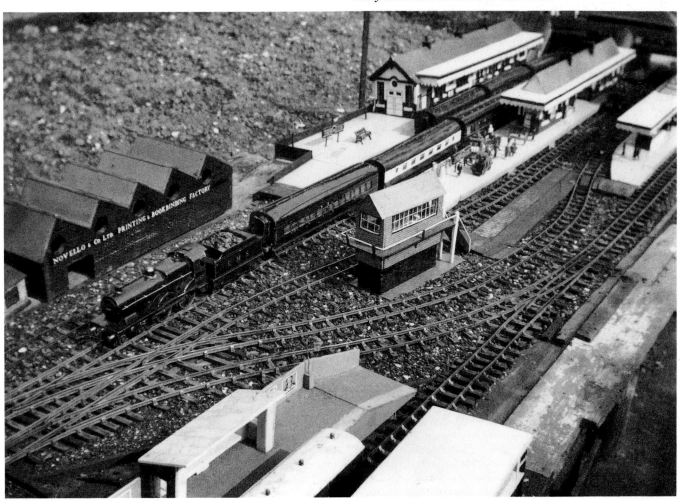

Bassett-Lowke Compound leaves the first Crewchester station in Kelvedon, hauling a rake of early Bassett-Lowke tinplate LMS coaches, bought from Mills Bros of Southampton Row, London, for 30/- (£1.50) each! 1952

Anxious not to lose such an opportunity, I telephoned Mr. Maskelyne to make an appointment, using as a flimsy pretext a little live steam 2-4-2 tank which in my ignorance I believed to be of Bassett-Lowke origin. The *Model Railway News* was at that time published by a firm named Percival Marshall, who were pioneers in producing books and pamphlets on the subject of model railways, and their offices were in Noel Street. Making my way there, I entered the hideous office-block, and was directed by the receptionist to take the lift to the third floor and look for the first door on my right on that landing. The almost Dickensian austerity of the place bore little relationship to the carpeted luxury of today's London offices, and the third floor landing was drab and dimly lit. I knocked on the door and a voice bade me enter.

Upon entering, I found myself in the sanctum of Mr. J.N. Maskelyne, who rose from behind his desk, a tall, slightly stooping figure, the long, scholarly face capped by a mane of hair brushed back severely behind the ears. His dress was invariably formal, a dark lounge-suit, and with a stand-up wing-collar, always with rounded corners. The spectacles were of a strictly utilitarian pattern, for he was not given to frills, but the spotless white handkerchief in his breast-pocket matched the immaculate cuffs. The welcoming smile was warm and friendly, and immensely dignified, quickly dispelling the feeling of slight panic I felt at taking up the time of a man who consorted with famous engineers, designers, and men of letters – a man who was honoured and respected wherever he went. What presumptuous pretext could I find for taking up his valuable time? I was offered a chair, and within minutes I was at my ease, for Maskelyne had that rare gift of giving everyone the impression that their company had made his day. He chatted easily, in a quiet, modulated voice which held both enthusiasm and authority, and when I nervously spoke of the garden railway I was building, he immediately showed interest, to the point of inviting me to write something for his magazine.

At that time, Maskelyne was editor not only of *Model Railway News*, in which he regularly wrote a column entitled "Railway Topics," but he was a broadcaster, writer, president of the Stephenson Locomotive Society, Technical Editor of the *Model Engineer*, and a lot else. I soon found that he was a good listener, and after a while I brought out my pathetic little steam engine. He took it from my hands, treating it as if I had offered him some rare antique and regarded it with affection.

"This is most interesting, Mr. Ray. What do you know of its origin, may I ask?" I confessed that I knew nothing, except that I rather thought it came from Bassett-Lowke. He set the engine on the desk before him, leaned back in his chair, and with fingers characteristically touching, finger-tip to finger-tip, he smiled and told me, "I think you will find that this is a Leeds model. Tell me, are you familiar with live-steam models?" When I confessed my total ignorance, he talked to me of pot-boilers, of slip-eccentric gears and many other mysteries of the steam engine, with such obvious relish that one would imagine he had only just discovered all these things for himself. Eventually, aware that I was taking up the time of a busy man, I took my leave, bearing the little 2-4-2 tank locomotive which was now hallowed by the laying on of hands of the master! He saw me to the lift, urging me to look in on him whenever I was in London, and I bore the engine home, where the little beast set fire to my baseboard, rendering it unfit for normal running for a week or more.

Many such visits followed, every one of which sent me away with some piece of newly-gleaned information, or sometimes an item of Gauge 0 interest which he insisted I accept. But what I gained from these encounters was far more valuable than any material gifts. He preached and practised only the highest standards of engineering and workmanship, yet his kindly nature was always tolerant of those who fell short of his ideals; his tone always encouraging rather than critical, with the effect of persuading his hearer to greater efforts of excellence. It was not until 1956 that the first article on Crewchester appeared in the *Model Railway News*, by which time the Ipswich Mark I version was in full swing.

The MODEL RAILWAY NEWS

A MAGAZINE OF RAILWAY MODELLING AND REAL RAILWAY TOPICS

Founded by: Percival Marshall, C.I.Mech.E. Edited by: J. N. Maskelyne, A.I.Loco.E.

Editorial and Publishing Offices:
13-16 FISHER STREET, LONDON, W.C.1

Single copies, post free, 7½d.

Annual Subscription, 7s. 6d.

Vol. 12. No. 133.   JANUARY, 1936.   Price 6d.

Notes of the Month

J. N. Maskelyne

Introducing Mr. J. N. Maskelyne

YOU must not blame Mr. Maskelyne for inserting his portrait in the first issue of the "M.R.N." to appear under his Editorship. Although he is so well known personally to model railway men in the London area, I want all our readers at home and aborad to meet their new Superintendent of the Line. Hence his portrait, and these personal notes. Mr. Maskelyne was educated at St. Paul's School, Hammersmith, and in the engineering department of King's College, Strand. He then served an apprenticeship in the Engineering Works of Messrs. Vickers, Ltd., at Erith, and subsequently joined the Staff of Messrs. Waygood-Otis Ltd., the well-known lift and escalator engineers. Here he rose to one of the chief positions in the Engineering Department. Since 1931, he has been working in a private capacity as consultant.

He is President and Chairman of the Stephenson Locomotive Society; has been Chairman of the Society of Model and Experimental Engineers, and is an Associate of the Institution of Locomotive Engineers. He has been known to the model railway world for many years past, through his lucid and well-informed writing on railway matters, as well as by lectures and judging at the meetings of various model railway clubs. As he is also a skilled model maker, I feel that the "M.R.N." is in for a long and successful run under his able guidance.

PERCIVAL MARSHALL

7

After the move to Ipswich in 1953 came a period of planning in which I was joined on frequent occasions by John Blair, who would make the 200-mile return trip to spend the weekend with me. The Kelvedon layout had been built originally at ground-level, but with the ground falling away as the line progressed down the garden, it ended up at table-top height. As I was in my thirties then, not long out of uniform and physically fit, stooping and bending presented no problems, but I did foresee that as the years passed, such contortions necessary to maintenance might become less than attractive, so it was agreed that the new railway would be at table-top height. As the ground in my new garden was almost level this presented no problems. It went without saying that the steel track must be replaced by brass, thereby constituting by far the biggest item in our budget, and as our stud of locomotives now included a Bassett-Lowke *Royal Scot* (parallel boiler, Fowler pattern), a *Duchess of Montrose* and *Princess Elizabeth* from the same stable, bought from Tyldesley and Holbrook of Manchester for the respective sums of £12 and £18, and in mint condition, we were unwilling to abandon spring-drive – the posh name for clockwork. Other engines and rolling stock had come our way, mainly due to my forays into the back-streets of the towns I worked in week by week, so we now possessed a reasonable array of models with which to run the railway.

Clockwork mechanisms fell broadly into two main categories; the 4-coupled type such as was found in the compound, and the larger 6-coupled type of 'Duchess', 'Princess', 'Scot'. The new line was therefore planned to suit the capabilities of these mechanisms, and worked more or less as follows. On a level track a four-coupled mechanism would haul a four-car train about 90ft, while a six-coupled mechanism would manage a six-car train for a distance of about 125ft. From the London terminus (City Road) in the garage, three tracks ran out into the garden to join a continuous circuit at Rockhill Junction. The circuit was double-track, running down the right-hand side of the garden, along the bottom, and up the other side where stood Crewchester station, some 90ft from City Road. Six-coupled engines could usually manage one complete circuit with a heavy train.

Most of my generation will be familiar with the famous shop at 112 High Holborn, London premises of Bassett-Lowke, but there was another fascinating model railway shop, only a few minutes' walk from there, in Southampton Row, the London home of Mills Bros., and run by two brothers named Spofforth. For quite a time the window of this shop held a display of quite complicated point-work which had at one time formed an imposing junction on someone's railway. It was ideal for the junction between the City Road spur and the main circuit on my line, so, by going without lunch for a few weeks, cadging a donation from John Blair, and cutting down the wife's housekeeping money, I was able to drive to London and return bearing this network of track, with the main line extremities resting on the back shelf of the car and the top of the fascia, and the spur in my left ear. The price-tag on this beautifully made point-work was £7.50!

The Spofforth brothers were responsible for other valuable additions to Crewchester, for it was from them that I bought our first Bassett-Lowke tinplate *Flying Scotsman* for £15 (consider that, you tinplate collectors of today!), four early Bassett-Lowke tinplate LMS bogie coaches for £1.50 each, complete with 1in cast-iron Mansell wheels, and this same shop built whatever turnouts we needed for the princely sum of £1.50 each – until a sudden increase to £5 put such things beyond us, and John Blair and I started thinking about the possibility of making our own

points. It was not until 1957, however, when the new extension to the main line down the centre of the garden to Ravensmoor and Inverblair was built that John undertook the manufacture of a large-radius double turnout. This, however, is jumping the gun, for in 1954 another significant event took place which affected the entire history of Crewchester and was responsible for shaping our plans for the new Ipswich layout.

During a visit to Walkers and Holtzappfel in Baker Street, I was talking to one of their staff whose name, I think, was Mallion. He asked me if I had ever heard of the Conway Model Railway in Harrow, and when I said I had not, he suggested that I contact them and arrange a visit, for they had a Gauge 0 clockwork railway with 75 locomotives, all carrying speed-governors, and the entire system run strictly according to prototype practice, to the extent that BR sent its students and apprentices there to learn how railways are run! The supremo of this club was a Mr. Joe Goadby-Griffiths, whom I contacted, followed by an invitation for John Blair and I to visit the railway on a non-running night, for on such nights there would be no opportunity for talk.

In due course John and I presented ourselves at a large house in Kenton, lying in the angle between the LMS (LNWR) and the LNER (GCR) main lines, and were welcomed by Joe. After the normal courtesies had been exchanged, we were taken to an office just inside the front hall, containing a telephone PBX and all the appurtenances of Control. Here, during running sessions Joe would sit, far removed from the large room upstairs where the action took place. From here we were led to the office where the drivers signed on, read the relevant notices of such things as permanent-way slacks, special workings, and would then collect their key before moving to the railway room and joining their engine.

Every locomotive had its own driver, who would walk round the layout with his charge, observing speed restrictions, and controlling the speed of his train. Should the engine's spring become fully unwound between stations there would be no question of taking out his key and giving a few extra turns, for the only place he was permitted to do this was at a water column. If he broke down between stations, he had to place a flag behind his train before going to the nearest signal box, of which there were five in that room, report the incident and await a rescue engine.

The pointwork which was displayed for so long in Mills Bros. shop in Southampton Row, 1954, now laid as the junction from the circuit to the garage on the new Ipswich layout in the same year.

The Conway Model Railway. Note the speed-control knurled wheel mounted just over the bunker of the tank engine, and the emu set which was driven from a full-size driver's console taken from an Underground train.

Downstairs, Joe would be organising the rescue and instructing the appropriate shed to send out a light engine to the scene of the failure. Time would be booked against the driver, and in the event of persistent failures of this kind, there would be a Court of Enquiry and the miscreant probably demoted to yard shunter. Promotion was not easy on that railway, and it might be some time before a driver so down-graded could regain his former role.

The signal boxes worked exactly as the full-size ones, with detailed logs of train-movements. I was told that the noise-level in that room when all five boxes were working was quite something, with all the block-bells ringing. The track was bullhead, secured by tiny wooden keys, which would often fall out, but, Joe told me, it did make replacement of worn track that much easier. The entire system, with one exception, ran (at that time) on spring-drive, and the exception was quite unusual. An electric multiple unit of Watford-Euston pattern was electrically driven, and this from a full-size tube-train console situated at one end of the room and acquired, we were told, from Golders Green Underground depot. As the driver was restricted to one position, beside the dead-man's handle, I wondered how the train was able to observe all signals, for it would pass out of view. It was pointed out to me that beside that controller was a panel of repeater signals, showing the progress of the train throughout its entire journey. All goods trains had been prepared before the session started, usually on a Wednesday evening before the Friday running night, each wagon having a way-bill attached to its solebar, for there was no haphazard running of freight trains; they were marshalled exactly as their prototype, to perform a specific job and follow logical routes and timings. Many of the members were knowledgeable about some aspect of railway practice and so a very high standard of operating was possible. The Bassett-Lowke Class J39 0-6-0 which runs at Crewchester today, came from one of the Conway members.

John Blair and I left that house in a daze, vowing that much of what we had seen would be incorporated in our new layout when I moved to Ipswich, and although we never went to the extremes practised by the Conway Club, nevertheless, all our engines carried correct headlamp codes, all trains bore a tail lamp, and trains were offered and accepted by block-bells and instruments, improvised from morse keys and door-bells at first, and then later by correct instruments obtained from BR.

Another memorable event took place in 1952 or 1953 – I cannot be certain of the exact year – when I was working in Swansea. I had read of the British Railways Model Railway which had been designed to travel round the country. BR Posters all over Swansea announced that it was being displayed in Swansea that week, so I lost no time in locating it and making my way there. It was the first time I had seen a fine-scale Gauge 0 railway, and it was impressive. Trains from all four regions were represented, and from the big control panel inside the barriers, a man was working the various movements. I soon got into conversation with him and his assistant, who, to our mutual astonishment proved to be a man who had served with me at 12 Group Fighter Command during the war, and in no time at all I found myself inside the barriers, with my war-time colleage introducing me to the boss – Ron Beddoes, who had built the exhibition railway and most of the locomotives.

After spending all my spare time there during that week I soon became familiar with the control panel and was able to take over in order to relieve Ron or his assistant. Subsequently, the layout came to Ipswich and Bury St Edmunds where not only did I do some volunteer relief-operating, but invited Ron round to Crewchester. Exactly the same thing happened a year or so later when I was working in Leeds and spotted the posters advertising the exhibition. This apparently irrelevant anecdote does, however, have a purpose. During that first week in Swansea, one evening

The first Crewchester station on the Ipswich layout 1954.

while I was operating the railway, a man carrying a brown paper parcel appeared at the barrier, where he was quickly recognised by Ron Beddoes and invited inside. "So" said Ron "you've got it at last!" The little man smiled and proceeded to unpack the parcel, brown wrapping paper giving way to layers of newspaper, and finally a bed of tissue paper. From this he produced a most beautiful Gauge 0 model of a GWR 'King' and handed it to Ron who, with reverential care, set it on the tracks of the loco yard close by the control panel.

"Come and look at this, Jack" he called. "Did you ever see anything so perfect? Makes my stuff look like rubbish!" (By my standards, Ron's models were superb!)

Ron then went on to explain: "Three years this has taken to build" and then in respectful tones he added "It is a Beeson model." I had never even heard the name of Beeson, and that day my education was improved. I saw, perhaps for the first time consciously, the heights of excellence which could be achieved in a Gauge 0 model. Thus was my introduction to one of the great masters of model locomotive engineering, and thirty-eight years later, in January 1989, I was lunching with Stanley Beeson, and mentioned the Swansea incident. He smiled and said "You know, I remember that engine – and that man." And he told me the man's name, which I have since forgotten.

Lest I may have given the impression that I now run Beeson-built locomotives, let me hasten to add that the occasion when I lunched with Stanley and Mrs. Beeson had been arranged by Colonel Hoare, with whom I was staying at the time. That day was

memorable, for once again a name I had learned to respect became a known face; the man behind the legend. Despite his 82 years and the fact that he walked with a stick, Beeson was tall and upright, with a quick sense of fun – not at all the austere figure I had pictured in my mind. He and Ronnie Hoare quite clearly enjoyed a close rapport and mutual respect. I asked Mrs. Beeson "Have you any idea of how highly your husband is regarded in the world of models?" Her reply was simple – "There is only one Stanley Beeson, isn't there?" This meeting took place in January 1989, but I must return to the 1950s, when that first Ipswich version of Crewchester was running in my back garden.

1956 was a momentous year. It was in that year that as a result of an article appearing in the *Model Railway News* I was contacted by a gentleman named Frank Pulham who lived in Walthamstow, and who, it appeared, had a considerable quantity of pre-war Gauge 0 items to dispose of, but which he wished to sell en bloc. A journey to Walthamstow brought me into contact with this remarkable character. Now well into his seventies, Frank Pulham stood erect and tall, well over six feet, white-haired, and very alert and enthusiastic. The collection for sale comprised all sorts of unusual models, such as a Tennant 2-4-0, an Ivatt 4-2-2, a Reid NBR 4-4-0 *Glen Roy*, a Bassett-Lowke *George the Fifth*, two *Duke of Yorks* and many others, plus items of rolling stock, etc. The asking price was £100 the lot! But it was the man himself who fascinated me, having been in turn a London bus-driver, a London policeman, and then fireman and driver out of Plaistow on the London, Tilbury & Southend Railway.

In his cockney voice, with its clear articulation, Frank Pulham told me many absorbing tales of the LT&SR, and the unusual thing about his speech was the utter absence of 'er' or 'um'. He never hesitated for a word. In 1908, at the White City Exhibition, he, then quite a youngster, was put in charge of the Whitelegg 4-4-2 Tilbury Tank on show there. For this duty he received no extra pay, and had to buy, out of his own money, a pair of slippers – ("Red slippers they was – corst me one-and-sixpence!") – before he was allowed to move about the immaculate engine. "Every lump of coal 'ad to be polished and laid out neat in the bunker and that engine had to be spotless. Old Mr. Whitelegg himself come along one day and went in under the engine – 'im an' his white gloves, and he wiped them over one of the big ends. When he come out from under he said to me "Not bad, Pulham – not bad. Keep it like that."

In moving the engine from Plaistow into the White City, one of the guard-irons had been broken off, so Frank was despatched, armed with his bus-fare, right across London to Plaistow shed where he was to draw a replacement from stores and bring it back across town so that it could be fitted to the damaged engine. Now, those guard irons were hefty things, bolted on to the front of the buffer-beam, and protruding like a great, curved horn outward and downward to almost rail-level – and they weighed a lot! Upon attempting to board a bus, the conductor refused to allow him on with that huge chunk of steel, and so he had perforce to walk the five miles or more, carrying that huge guard-iron over his shoulder, and all he got for his pains was a complaint that he had taken so long.

On another of my visits to Frank, he spoke of his hero, whose name he pronounced 'Mr. Marsk-e-line', enthusing over the many fine locomotive drawings of 'JNM'. The centenary of the LT&SR had recently taken place, with one of the Tilbury Tanks done out in the original livery. Frank had been on Southend station, as had Maskelyne, and the two had met, briefly. "Real gent, that man is; treated me almost like an old friend." But Frank went on to mention a recent article by J.N. Maskelyne on the Tilbury Tanks, and, according to Frank, he had got one small detail wrong in his description of the livery. "Now, Jack" said Frank, "don't you ever mention this to Mister Marsk-e-line when you see him; he knows more about steam engines than anyone I know, and he is always accurate. "But," he went on, "he describes the casing of the donkey pump and cylinders as being black. Well, strictly speakin' they wasn't black – they was dark grey, 'cos they was made of what was called German metal – a dark grey."

A week or so later I was once again in Maskelyne's office in Noel Street and mentioned my visits to Frank Pulham, telling him how Frank remembered meeting him on Southend station. Maskelyne leaned back in his chair, smiling. "I remember the occasion very well, Mr. Ray – and Mr. Pulham – a quite remarkable character. He had actually driven on the Tilbury Line." Here, I fear I betrayed Frank's confidence, for I told him of how, when we were discussing the article on the Tilbury Tanks, Frank had suggested that there was a slight inaccuracy. "You describe the casing of the cylinders and donkey-pump as being black, whereas Frank . . ."

"Just a moment, Mr. Ray – just a moment; I am much obliged to Mr. Pulham, for he is perfectly correct. Those casings were made of German metal, so they would in fact not be black, but grey. Will you, when you next see Mr. Pulham, give him my thanks." It seemed that one just could not really catch that man out in matters of locomotive detail. Later, I recounted the interview to Frank, who was torn between embarrassment that I had broken his

Left –
The author with Frank Pulham in August 1957 and North British Railway Glen Roy *from Frank's collection.*

confidence and pleasure in receiving that message of gratitude from his hero. "One of nature's gentlemen, that he is!" was Frank Pulham's comment.

This account of J.N. Maskelyne can best be completed by two more sidelights upon him, the first illustrating the sense of fun which lay beneath the rather formal appearance. An article on Crewchester had been published, illustrated by photographs, one of which showed the long, sweeping curve of tracks to the south of Crewchester station – and which Maskelyne had christened "the Stafford curve" – beside which stood the engine-sheds. A Hornby tender had been carelessly left in the ballast between the loco roads and the main line, and this had brought comment in the form of a letter from a reader Mike Huggard in Ireland. At the head of the article I had plagiarised Lewis Carol thus:

"The time has come" the walrus said
"To talk of many things –
"Of gears and cogs and speed-controls
And whether tanks have springs"

In his letter, addressed to the Editor, *Model Railway News*, Mr. Huggard wrote

"'Twas brillig and the lithey lokes
Did wrig and slidle tround the rack;
They wuffed and pistled, croaned with groaks,
And what is more, bame cack."

and he ended his letter with "And now, Mr. Ray, though it is a tender subject, how did you come to leave that beautiful Hornby tender sitting right there on the ballast between the rails, where no rails are?

Yours faithfully
M.K. Huggard   Co Wicklow."

As he showed me the letter, Maskelyne, obviously enjoying the situation, asked me if I would care to reply here and now, and he would publish both letter and reply in the next issue. He sent for his secretary who took her seat beside him behind the desk, and she waited stoically for a lengthy reply. I dictated it to her as follows

Dear Sir,

Touché!

Yours faithfully
J.L. Ray

Maskelyne laughed and said "Would that all correspondents were as brief and to the point!" Finally, I would quote in full a letter I received from Maskelyne just after Christmas 1958, for it is typical of the man.

The picture in the Model Railway News which prompted Mr. Huggard's amusing letter.

East Lodge
Midgham
Reading, Berks

31st December 1958

Dear Mr. Ray,

Thank you so much for your letter, Christmas card, and good wishes. This letter brings you and all your associates of the Crewchester Model Railway my cordial greetings and warmest good wishes for a very successful and enjoyable New Year.

While, as you say, my personal preference is that railway models should be accurate, I fully appreciate that fine-scale modelling is available and possible to only a few enthusiasts. If fine-scale modelling was the rigid rule, rather than the exception, there would be far less railway modelling than there is, simply because modern domestic amenities so seldom permit enough space being available for any reasonable fine-scale layout. The actual craftsmanship required for fine-scale modelling is not so very different from coarse-scale; it takes rather more time, owing to the greater care necessary for fine-scale work.

No sir! I am perfectly satisfied with coarse-scale modelling, so long as the models represent their prototypes with reasonable accuracy and proportion, and are operated in a railway-like manner.

After all, what you and your colleagues have achieved on the Crewchester Line is just about ideal. Most of the photographs I have seen of your efforts are thoroughly convincing; with the unavoidable exception of the track, there is nothing that really looks out of proportion, and the general effect is always very pleasing. The photograph on your Christmas card is sufficient evidence of this; and if all coarse-scale model railways were of this standard there would be no need to complain! What I object to on any model railway is careless, clumsy workmanship in the construction, proportion, and arrangement of the various components that make up the whole; but even in this, one must make allowance for the exigencies of space.

You have got the right idea; keep it up! There is nothing on the Crewchester Line of which you need be ashamed.

I am glad my namesake* is now behaving himself properly, thus emulating what his 'prototype' tries to do!

With kindest regards
Very sincerely yours
J.N. Maskelyne.

* With his full approval, I had named a free-lance Bing 4-6-0 locomotive "J.N. MASKELYNE" which ran right to the end of clockwork days at Crewchester.

I often wonder what Maskelyne would have made of some of today's model railway publications, with not only the new techniques in printing but the woefully lowered standards of literacy prevailing in so many articles, often overlooked or ignored by the Editorial Chair. He himself was an extremely articulate and fastidious man; qualities which were abundantly obvious in his magazines and writings which he produced before, during, and after the war, in conditions of paper-shortage and other daunting problems, and with few of the amenities now at the command of the publisher. To know 'JNM' was not only a privilege; it was inspiring, for invariably one left him with the feeling of having consorted with a great gentleman. His genuine interest in what others were doing or trying to achieve encouraged one to greater efforts and a little more care.

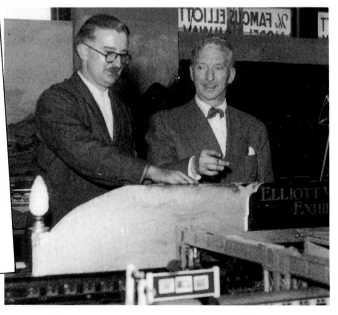

Harold Elliott (left) and A.N. Other. Circa 1952.

Photographs of the prototype are invaluable for modelling purposes and I have selected three here that record the railway as it was. Above is the westward view from Exeter St. Davids in 1973. A forest of Great Western semaphores of all types persuade the eye that a magnificent 'King' will approach from Penzance at any moment with a Paddington bound express.

Taken twenty years ago, Kettering Midland station (right) has survived almost all the neglect shown to the majority of British railway stations as well as a serious attempt to demolish it and replace it with a sterile modern structure.

Below is Torrington, Devon where once I would join an ancient two car train for Barnstaple headed by a Southern M7 0-4-4T. My 1973 view shows the daily china clay train waiting at platform 1, now just an echo of earlier days. Even the milk traffic still survived as evidenced by the tankers in the goods shed road.

Above:
A much-modified Bing 4-6-0 of the early 1920s, slightly 'Robinsonised' by Jack Ray and named J. N. Maskelyne. In his letters, Mr Maskelyne would sometimes ask after his namesake at Crewchester! These Bing mechanisms were quite the most powerful and smooth running clockwork 6-coupled types of their age.

Below:
Made for a cigarette coupon scheme by Bassett-Lowke, this freelance 4-4-0 lay in a direct line of descent from the old Duke of York 4-4-0s, again made by Bassett-Lowke for B.D.V. Cigarettes, for 50p each. This particular model was named 'PRINCE CHARLES' and appeared in the post-1939-45 war era.

In sharp contrast to Maskelyne, yet warmly remembered, is the figure of Harold Elliott, showman extraordinary, who during the 1950s held court at the Tower, Blackpool with his model railway, composed almost exclusively of Bassett-Lowke proprietary items. Not for Harold the aesthetic perfectionism of the usual model railway enthusiast, but rather the Punch-and-Judy approach, with 'Sammy the Shunter' pulling the children in to laugh and scream at the antics of the naughty little engine. I got to know Harold well, and had great respect for his undoubted ability as a showman. It is easy to sneer at what may appear to be unworthy of our hobby, but who knows how many small children who delighted in that fairground Gauge O model railway went on to want a layout of their own? 'Sammy the Shunter' was undoubtedly the precursor of 'Thomas the Tank Engine' – and let him who dares denigrate Thomas!

Normal operation would be suspended periodically so that Sammy could do his piece, and Harold would explain that Sammy (an 0-6-0T) was a naughty little engine who would not do as he was told. He had a face on his smoke-box door, and his place was the shunting yard. Fancying himself as a main line express engine, Sammy should escape, pursued by Harold, who tried in vain to persuade him to return to his duties in the yard. It caused great excitement and hilarity among the very young, but for the older children, Harold had another trick. He would invite two or three lads inside the barrier, show them the controller, and then invite them to drive a seven-car train into a station which would accommodate only four coaches. The puzzle was to stop the train so that all passengers could alight on to the platform, and it was *not* a corridor train. Occasionally, some smart lad would spot that the first two and the last vehicles were in fact full-brake or parcels vans, and bring the train in so that the four passenger vehicles were in the platform.

Running a model railway is all very well as a hobby, but to do it from 10.30am to 6.00pm seven days a week for ten weeks must remove some of the gilt from the gingerbread. Hot, sunny days would see the railway room deserted in the afternoons, with people preferring the beach, and sometimes I would collect Harold, who would lock up the exhibition room, and come for a spin to somewhere like Fleetwood. He seemed grateful for someone who could talk about other things than model railways and on some evenings I would drive him home where, with 'Titch', his wife, we would enjoy a fish-and-chip supper, for Blackpool provides the best fish-and-chips in the world (or so they say in Blackpool!). One evening, we were discussing his show and I suggested a slightly more ambitious scenario for that digression, whereby Sammy demands to work on the main line, and is eventually given an express train to haul. The plot was very obvious; how Sammy finds the work too much for him, repents of his folly, and returns to his yard, but not until he has been chased round the layout by Harold with a rolled-up newspaper.

Just as in a pantomime, children love to shriek out ''He's BEHIND you,'' so they would scream ''He's in the tunnel!'' The engine could be controlled by a foot-pedal, thus leaving Harold with both hands free. And so the play would move to its end with Harold pointing the moral – that it is unwise to try to live above your station in life!

1957. William Appleby, the well-known broadcaster to schools for many years who presented the Monday morning programme on radio 'Listening Together', seen here at Crewchester with Walter Mayhew, with young Stuart Ray, aged seven.

Later on, when lunching with Roland Fuller of Bassett-Lowke, Roland told me that Harold was the bane of their life, for he would delay sending in engines for repair until the flanges had worn so thin that they sheared off. After leaving Blackpool, Harold took his railway to Scarborough, and then to Brighton, where his layout gave pleasure to thousands of holiday-makers.

Yet another well-known character belongs to those years of the 1950s. Many thousands of youngsters who attended primary school between 1948 and 1958 will remember the radio programme 'Listening Together' presented by the popular William Appleby. William (Pip to his friends) was not only a musician and historian, but a keen railway and model railway enthusiast. In his spare time he studied signalling and unofficially qualified as a Class I Relief Signalman, just as a pastime. When I was working in South Yorkshire I would lunch with Pip in Doncaster before driving off to Wath-on-Dearne to do an hour or so train-spotting. He also visited Crewchester, and I was able to help him add to his growing collection of Gauge O clockwork locomotives which he ran on his layout in his home at Skipton. There must be many middle-aged people today who will remember with affection those Monday morning broadcasts (all presented 'live' in those days) with Pip's cheery ''Hullo, schools! Now – everyone sit up straight and listen while Miss Avis plays the tune we learned last week.''

The 1950s were indeed rich in memories of so many people who played some part in the development of Crewchester, and I have dealt so far with only a few. But before introducing others who walked on to the scene, let me try to describe the scene itself as it was in the mid-50s; and for this – a new chapter.

THE CREWCHESTER MODEL RAILWAY CLUB
and the
GAUGE 0 GUILD

The story of Crewchester is rather like a mountain range; high peaks of spectacular progress and activity alternating with valleys of routine, maintenance, and enjoyable operating. The middle 1950s saw one of the highest peaks in the chain.

John Blair and I, inspired by our visit to the Conway Model Railway had returned to Ipswich and the new Ipswich layout had been built and was operating tolerably well. The glaring faults in planning were yet to manifest themselves, and all seemed to be going smoothly. However, by reason of the distance between us, John could visit but infrequently, and with my work taking me away from home during term-time, progress was restricted mainly to holiday periods. Rudimentary block-bells, improvised from door-bells and morse-keys had been installed between City Road and Crewchester, obviating the necessity to yell at each other across the garden every time a train was offered, but we looked forward to something a little more professional in the future. John and I had spent a number of nights in Hatfield No. 2 signal box on the East Coast main line, thereby acquiring a taste for proper block instruments and more-or-less correct procedure, but it was to be several years before such luxuries were forthcoming.

It was in 1954 that I conceived the idea of trying to form some sort of club, for the railway was becoming far too large for just two people to operate comfortably, so I canvassed the local secondary school for boys interested in railways, with the result that thirty thirteen-year-olds arrived at my house one Saturday. A system of training in railway practice was initiated, somewhat on the lines of the Conway MRC practice, dividing boys between signalmen and drivers, in which role they were able to graduate through a number of tests until they arrived at the dizzy height of 'supervisor', which entitled them to organise and supervise a running session in my absence, a heavy responsibility. Having qualified in one role, a member could re-train in the other; in fact this was a requisite of a supervisor; he must be competent in all aspects of running the timetables, as well as being trustworthy, for security was an important factor. It is worth remembering that in 1954 steam was still dominant on our railways and boys were familiar with steam engines and travelled behind them, for the family car was not yet available to any but the moderately well-to-do families.

From about Easter to October, or even November, every weekend would see a band of operators running the trains; school holidays would see almost daily attendance. It took about two years for a member to qualify as a supervisor and not all made that grade, or even wanted to; they preferred to be the hewers of wood and drawers of water. But the social side of the club rapidly increased in importance. Visits were made to signalboxes and stations, engine sheds, and other model railways; winter meetings were arranged with slide and film shows, or talks by experts on railway practice. By far the most popular subject was the Ministry official reports of major railway disasters, many of which make more exciting reading than a detective novel.

Many an amusing anecdote could be told about those early days, but one extraordinary incident will suffice. Living in Thorpe-le-Soken, some twenty miles from Ipswich, was Frank Vaux, whose wonderful Gauge 0 layout in the cellar of the Old Mill House represented a Caledonian Railway system. Frank would often drop in to join in a running session, and on one such occasion, when I was expecting him, I told the boys "Put on a good show today, for Colonel Vaux is coming." In due course Frank arrived, and the two of us stood in the middle of the garden, watching the boys operate the trains. As one train ran down from the garage towards the bottom of the garden, I noticed that it had no tail-lamp, and immediately I was faced with a problem; did I draw attention to it and thereby possibly embarrass the boy who had despatched the train, or should I keep quiet and hope that my guest had not noticed the missing lamp?

The train ran right round the garden to arrive safely at Crewchester, so I walked over to the operator there and asked him to ring City Road and report that the train had arrived without a tail-lamp. Colonel Vaux looked on with interest as the ensuing conversation became a trifle heated, the City Road operator insisting that they had placed a tail lamp on the train. Meanwhile, Crewchester were about to send an up train in the opposite directon to City Road, but I asked that this train should be delayed until the missing tail-lamp had been found. A sudden shout from City Road announced that it had been found; it was in fact still on the bracket of the rear coach of the down train, which had become detached in the tunnel leading from City Road out into the garden, and was standing right in the path of the up train which could have been on its way. The opportunity to preach the gospel of "rules is rules" with this dramatic example of just why tail lamps are statutory, was too good to be missed, and our visitor was duly impressed. But Frank Vaux was most reluctant to be persuaded that the whole thing had not been staged just to impress him.

The newly formed Crewchester Model Railway Club, May 1955. John Blair is on the extreme left, and my step-son, David, can be seen towering over the scene at the back.

E.A.D.T.

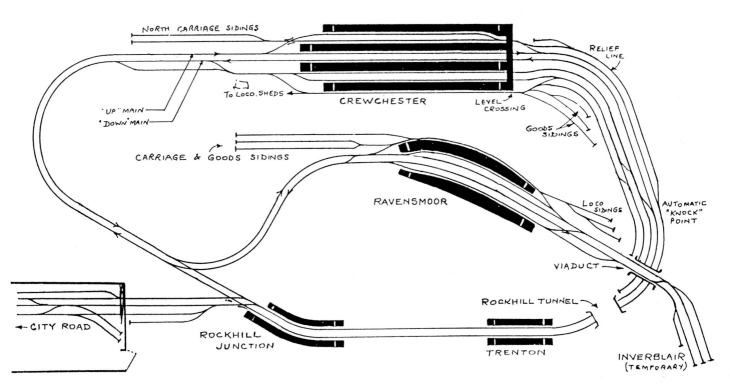

NORTH CARRIAGE SIDINGS

RELIEF LINE

"UP" MAIN
"DOWN" MAIN

To LOCO. SHEDS

CREWCHESTER

LEVEL CROSSING

GOODS SIDINGS

CARRIAGE & GOODS SIDINGS

RAVENSMOOR

LOCO SIDINGS

AUTOMATIC "KNOCK" POINT

VIADUCT

CITY ROAD

ROCKHILL JUNCTION

ROCKHILL TUNNEL

TRENTON

INVERBLAIR (TEMPORARY)

The first Ipswich layout 1954 to 1961.

Jack Holbrook, 1964.

These were happy days, with the rolling stock gradually being added to from various sources, one of which deserves special mention. The well-known shop of Tyldesley and Holbrook stood in Deansgate, Manchester, a true Mecca for the model railway enthusiast, and presided over by Jack Holbrook, a quietly-spoken Mancunian who made his visitors welcome, whether they bought anything or not. Many a day I would call there just to pass the time of day and sometimes we would cross the road together to the Kardomah cafe to enjoy a quiet cup of coffee and a chat. When finances permitted I would buy items from him, ranging from boxes of Dinky toy human figures to coaches, vans, and the occasional locomotive, for clockwork engines were still fairly easy to find – second-hand, of course – in those days, and Holbrook's prices were always fair. For more than twenty years I went to Jack Holbrook for all my track parts, which he obtained through his friend, Boyd-Carpenter of Baslow. Whenever I lacked some vital component such as bell-cranks I would write to Manchester and a parcel would come back by return with several alternative samples, inviting me to take my pick and return what I did not want. His phraseology was a trifle dated, and pleasant to see, for his letters would read "I thank you for the favour of your esteemed order –" – and he was punctilious about sending a receipt. On two or three occasions I went to his lovely house in Hale Barns where, in the garage, he had a Gauge 0 railway. The remarkable thing was that although he was much older than I was, he kept his railway up to date, gradually replacing his fine steam-outline engines with diesel and electric.

One day in the spring of 1956 I was standing in the doorway of his shop, enjoying the warm sunshine, when he said "Have you heard about this new association they are trying to form for Gauge

0?" When I told him I had not, he told me that an Edinburgh solicitor named Loch-Kidston had suggested that Gauge 0 people might get together to form some sort of group, club, or society. Loch-Kidston used to write under the nom-de-plume of 'Auld Reekie', but I had never met him. Jack Holbrook gave me the name and address of the man who was actually doing the spade-work in getting interested people together, one Harold Bower, and in due course I contacted Harold and was told that an exploratory meeting was to be held at an address in Euston Square during the summer of 1956.

On the appointed day, John Blair and I made our way to Euston Square, found the rather shabby railway buildings, probably used by drivers and crews for lodging turns, and made our way up the bare stairs to an equally bare room, its unadorned walls whitewashed, and its only furniture a few steel-framed chairs, and a table where Harold Bower sat in splendid and lonely isolation. Some thirty men were sitting, chatting, and John and I joined them to await events. As I was already holding office in my own professional association, it was a rare treat to sit back and watch someone else do all the work, but my complacency was short-lived. Harold rose to his feet and suggested that before any formal business was attempted it might be a good thing for everyone to stand up in turn, announce his name, and what his interest was in Gauge 0. This device effectively broke the ice and produced an atmosphere of camaraderie.

Harold then announced that before any formal business could be done it was necessary to find a Chairman (President), a Treasurer, and a quorum of committee members. Someone asked why the instigator of this group, Mr. Loch-Kidston, was not present, but that question remained unanswered for all time because that gentleman never appeared at any meeting. Harold Bower then said "We must first of all elect a Chairman and then work out an 'ad hoc' agenda, so may I suggest that Jack Ray might be persuaded to occupy this position? He has written several articles recently on Gauge 0 topics and his name will be familiar to many prospective members – –" Thus did I have greatness thrust upon me, and became the first Chairman/President of the Gauge 0 Guild, an event which in retrospect I regard with some pride, but at the time neither I nor anyone else in that room had any idea of just how the Guild would grow to the size it is today.

John Blair found himself appointed Hon. Treasurer, and that first balance sheet makes interesting reading today, showing how we were scratching around in an effort to raise £25 capital with which to launch the Guild. It was a timely move, for such an Association was sorely needed. The trade had all but abandoned Gauge 0; Bassett-Lowke, Mills Bros., the Leeds Model Co, Walkers and Holtzappfel, et al had either disappeared or had turned to other products, leaving Bonds o' Euston Road the sole survivors of Gauge 0 supplies. Even Bonds needed persuading that we meant business, for in an interview with Mr. Phillips Senior, their manager, in 1956, I was told in no uncertain terms that this new Guild would not last, was merely a flash in the pan, that within a year or so it would start to sag and then collapse as the initial enthusiasm wore off. I had gone to ask Mr. Phillips to reconsider his decision not to renew the mould for making diecast slide-on rail chairs, for if those chairs went off the market we would be without any source of supply. Possibly the first instance of the Guild being able to show its teeth was when, through the Guild, I rustled up orders for 20,000 chairs, thereby convincing Bonds that we meant business. The new mould was made, and today, 35 years later, those chairs are still selling well!

Those days spent working in Manchester brought me another good friend, Mr. Cox, the manager of Bassett-Lowke's Manchester shop. He it was who initiated me into the easiest way of changing a spring in a clockwork mechanism – a painful, dangerous, and often sanguinary job for the amateur.

The same year as that in which the Gauge O Guild was formed saw perhaps the most important encounter in our history, for it was then that I first met John Hart of Surbiton, thereby striking up a close friendship which lasted for 25 years. An article entitled 'M.I.C. in 0 Gauge' had appeared in the *Model Railway News*, and had been seen by John who told me later that he realised that he and I were both doing much the same thing; running a Gauge O model railway with the help of a band of young men and boys, so why not arrange a meeting? This was done, and a party of boys accompanied John to Ipswich for a session at Crewchester, thereby starting what was to become a close association beween the two clubs, one clockwork and the other outside-third. I had in fact heard of John in connection with an exhibition model railway which ran for a few years at Chessington Zoo, in association with Rob Dettmar. This was in fact, the very first stud-contact model railway ever put on show to the general public.

If the 1950s were a peak in the story of Crewchester, the year 1956 was the very summit, for three enduring friendships were forged in that year which were to have a profound influence on the course of my model railway; John Hart, George Hinchcliffe, and Arthur Dewar. Before the dramatis personae becomes too involved, let me introduce George Hinchcliffe and Arthur Dewar. When I first met George at the inaugural meeting of the Gauge 0 Guild (when he assumed the role of our first Trade Liaison Officer) George was a schoolmaster in Lincolnshire, so over the years that followed we met in two separate spheres of activity – in the world of education, and in that of model railways. George is one of those incredible people who seem to have discovered a 25-hour day and still finds it inadequate, and was a prime mover in the establishment of the now famous Gainsborough Model Railway Society which in fact became established as a youth group recognised by the local council.

The Society took over an abandoned primary school in Gainsborough and proceeded to build one of the most audacious layouts I have ever encountered, covering the entire first-floor of the school. The main hall contained an imposing model of King's Cross station, York Road, Ferme Park goods depot, Gasworks tunnels, and the lines running down to Moorgate (since removed). Running through other rooms, the line passed through Peterborough, Grantham and ultimately to Leeds. Other intermediate stations, most of them block posts, were operated by correct block procedure, each worked by a member of the Society, and with hidden loops under the baseboard where trains could 'consume time' until they were due to reappear. The entire system was two-rail, fine-scale, and a bewildering assortment of trains ran over the line, from suburban Class N2 0-6-2Ts with quad-art sets to Gresley's Pacifics and other top link locomotives handling the more important expresses such as the magnificent 'Yorkshire Pullman'.

Almost every conceivable type of engine of LNER and GCR origin could be seen here, many of them built by George. Very soon I found myself becoming involved with this band of merry men and became a sort of country member, and making many new friends there. One man, Fred Newman, who seems to have made more Gauge 0 coaches than most of us have ever seen, including the trains running at Gainsborough, started to build coaches for Crewchester, most of which are still running today. These are made from card, which material, says Fred, is the strongest stuff for such work. Metal, he tells us, if dropped will buckle; plastic will shatter; wood is clumsy. Card, properly treated with shellac, laminated and shaped, well constructed, will just bounce if dropped! I hesitate to put this theory to a practical test, but the fact remains that Fred's coaches, some of them built as long ago as 1954, are still running at Crewchester.

The engine built by George Hinchcliffe in 1958, Edward Thompson, *hauling a train of Fred Newman LNER teak coaches.*

The Down 'Raven Pullman' approaching Crewchester Junction, headed by A4 Golden Eagle, *with Pullman cars from the Gainsborough Model Railway Society.*

George Hinchcliffe soon made a return visit to Crewchester, and within minutes of arrival, was working City Road as if he had designed it – even in the unfamiliar medium of clockwork! Whilst spending a day with us in Ipswich, George expressed a desire to build an engine for Crewchester – at cost-of-materials. We decided on an LNER Pacific, leaving the choice to George and less than two years later, in 1958, he produced a fine clockwork model of a Thompson Class A2/3 *Edward Thompson*, first of all exhibiting it at the Central Hall Easter show that year, where it attracted much attention. Indeed, almost too much attention for George's liking, for he had charged me a mere £26 for that engine, and had no wish to make any more of that model. However, one admirer at Central Hall, hearing that George was the builder of *Edward Thompson*, asked him if he would build him one. George, not anxious to take on more work, trebled the price, whereupon the man took out his cheque-book there and then! *Edward Thompson*, now modified to 2-rail, is still running, thirty-two years later.

On one visit to Gainsborough, while I was busy cleaning track, I overheard a member say that the Pullman set was going to be replaced by a new set of five cars built by Fred Newman, so I asked George if there were any possibility of my buying them. "You can have the bodies" he told me "but not the bogies; you'll have to find the bogies yourself. But you can have the bodies when we get the new set, for £3 each." Some years later, that new set was introduced, but while George was away, a member of the committee was approached by a visitor who asked if he might purchase the five redundant cars, and the member, ignorant of George's casual verbal agreement with me, accepted the offer of more than three times the price quoted to me. When George returned and heard of the transaction, he immediately cancelled it, saying "Those Pullmans were promised to Jack Ray years ago, and he is going to have them – at £3 each." So it was that the Pullman set came to Ipswich, running there until the demise of clockwork,

as the 'Raven Pullman'.

It was during that first year at Gainsborough that George Hinchcliffe told me that he wanted me to see what he described as a 'miniature Gainsborough' and so we drove from Gainsborough to the village of Saxilby, which lies between Gainsborough and Lincoln. The village chemist was Arthur Dewar, to whom I was introduced, and who led us up into his stock-rooms where I was shown a Gauge 0 model railway based upon Blair Athol station, with a continuous circuit of double track. A variety of trains ran here, with LMS Black Five and Stanier 2-6-4T models running alongside engines in Highland Railway livery, such as *Ben Alder* – one of the 'Small Bens', still with its bogie tender – and a fine model of the Jones Goods 4-6-0. For nearly 25 years after that first meeting, I stayed with Arthur when my work took me to Lincolnshire, and I soon discovered that this quiet, unassuming man was not only extremely well-read in a wide variety of subjects, but had an abiding love of all things Scottish; hardly surprising with a name like Dewar!

It was from Arthur that I first heard of the name Parley. Rev Parley, it appeared, had been a parson in the same Durham town where Arthur's father, a doctor, practised, and the families were friendly. Parley eventually went to the living of Tivetshall St. Mary in Norfolk, where he had built a huge Gauge 0 railway, operated by clockwork, running through its kitchen-garden behind the Rectory, and also through outbuildings. It was a GNR/NER line representing the East Coast Route from King's Cross to Edinburgh. With none of today's kits or ready-made locomotives available to him, Parley built his own, often working in slightly over-scale dimensions to accommodate the larger clockwork mechanisms. This huge layout was operated by all manner of people, from porters to parsons, and I understand that Parley was reprimanded by his Bishop for running trains when he ought to have been running his parish!

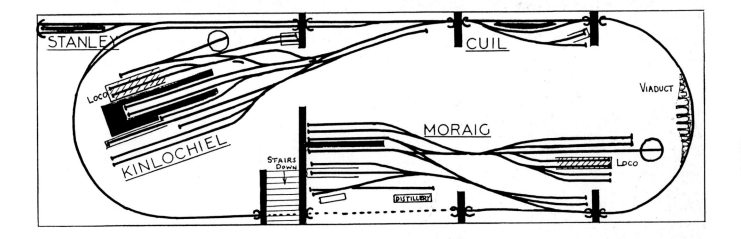

A Highland Railway layout by Arthur Dewar 1985.

Very soon after I first met him, Arthur dismantled the Blair Athol layout in favour of one representing the line from Kyle of Lochalsh to Strome Ferry, via Plockton, at the same time disposing of his LMS engines in order to build up a stud of Highland locomotives. The period he aimed at was the first decade of this century, making possible such engines as 'Barney' goods, 'Lochs', Small and Large 'Bens', a 2-4-0T *Breadalbane* and other such typical engines of the period. Later, when he retired, Arthur built a house with a first-floor room entirely devoted to his final railway, again Highland, but with a continuous circuit running round the walls, with two opposing terminal stations inside the circuit. With the clever use of both relief and backdrop scenery, Arthur has created a beautiful Highland setting against which his trains may run. On many an occasion he has sent me home bearing some item of goods stock which he has either made for Crewchester, or donated from his own store.

There is one story which, although out of chronological order here, does serve to link all three railways – Arthur's, John Hart's, and mine. During the late 1960s I was operating John's Midland & Southern Counties Joint Railway in Surbiton, and was working Oakleigh on the branch. A train was sent down to me from Broadway, headed by what I can only call a perfect cow of an engine; one I had never seen before. In LMS black, the engine was an ex-HR Drummond 'Castle' class 4-6-0, and whatever motor it contained was clearly useless, for it knew only two speeds – stop and full-speed. Upon enquiring of John as to the origin of this horrible engine, I was informed that he had picked it up cheaply, hoping to make it run – some day. I heard no more of the matter until some years later, when visiting Arthur Dewar, who had acquired a nice-looking Highland Railway 'Castle' class 4-6-0 named *Blair Castle*, finished in plain HR green. Arthur had been on a visit to Surbiton, had seen the black 4-6-0 and, like me, had asked John what was to become of it. The outcome of this visit was that John Hart fitted a new RM motor to the engine, Arthur Dewar bought it from him, had the wheels skimmed down to 29.2mm back to back, the black LMS livery removed to be replaced by the green Highland colours, and was running it on his own Highland Railway.

The final episode in this saga took place many years later, during the 1980s in fact, when I had gone over to 12v electric power. I had been showing Arthur some of Barrie Walls' work on my newly converted locos, including a fine scratch-built Class N7 0-6-2T, which Arthur admired. Did I think Barrie would build an engine for him? Arthur explained that he wanted a Highland Railway 'Castle', and when I pointed out that he already had one he replied that, nice as it was, it was not up to the standard of his other engines. The result was that Barrie Walls did build that Castle for Arthur, which left him with an unwanted model. I had always admired that Drummond design, and in the end I bought the engine from Arthur, had it re-converted to 28mm b-b wheel dimensions, added number plates and works plate, and the engine now runs at Crewchester. It has no logical role to play in my south-of-the-border railway, but I like the engine, and that is the end of the matter.

But the RM motor was not entirely compatible with my own control system, and a great friend of mine, Eddie Bye, who wanted an RM motor, offered to fit a JH motor in exchange for the RM. He phoned me from his home in Kent one day – "Has that Castle engine of yours ever been through John Hart's hands?" When I asked why he wanted to know he replied "I don't know, Jack – but that engine has John's handwriting all over it. I just get the feeling that it has been to him at some time or other." I told Eddie the full story. He said "Yes. I thought so – you can recognise John's workmanship anywhere."

I think that John would ask for no better epitaph than that.

But to return to the 1950s and the events of 1956, when John and I first met, he aged 50, and I 40, I doubt if any one person has had more influence on my model railway activities and interests than John.

He was trained as an engineer and chose the profession of model engineering, which he practised from his home in Surbiton, specialising in Gauge 0. He would strongly deny any special skills in his chosen medium, saying "Compared to Bernard Miller or Stanley Beeson I am merely a hack." Hack or not, John's ideas worked, and he had a favourite saying "I don't care how good it looks; if it doesn't work, it doesn't interest me." When faced with any engineering problem, he would sit back, stare at the object in question, be it locomotive, track, or other component, and sit silently for some time. Then, as if emerging from a trance he would

April 1967. John Hart at Polehampton on the Midland & Southern Counties Joint Railway, testing a Bassett-Lowke Stanier 2-6-4T from the Crewchester stud which he had re-wheeled and greatly modified and improved, before returning it to Crewchester.

say "All right – leave it with me; I'll think about it." In the fullness of time he would return the problem-child, saying "Take that and try it – and let me know." Invariably the thing worked. Never did I hear John use words such as "What you ought to do is – –". But, conversely, tell John something was impossible and his moustache would twitch ominously; he would go silent and the chances were that sooner or later, John would have achieved the "impossible." Many are the examples I could quote, but one or two will suffice.

One evening I was working in my favourite place, Oakleigh, the terminus of the branch, and John, sitting behind me, was operating Westhaven. During a lull in the proceedings he said "How do you like this, Jack?" I looked round to see him driving an engine on to the turntable, after which it moved slowly to the ash-pits. As it stood there, the heap of ash beside the engine began to give off a red glow. Now, an unspoken rule between John and myself was never to enthuse overmuch, but try to go one better. "Very good, John" I said "but where's the smoke?" No reply came, but the eyes regarded me steadily and the moustache twitched! The following week we were in the same position, and I watched an engine move to those ash-pits. The ash glowed – and then a thin spiral of smoke started to rise from the heap. Game, set, and match to John!

During one of our discussions on my Bassett-Lowke A3, *Flying Scotsman*, I mentioned how much I disliked the coarse steam-roller, small diameter bogies, which to my mind, ruined the otherwise pleasant appearance of the model. "Trouble is" I told John, "it is impossible to fit scale size bogies on that model; there is just not sufficient clearance under the cylinders." John stopped what he was doing. "Oh?" said he "And who told you that?" I played my trump card. "Harry Franklin, a Director of Bassett-Lowke, when I lunched with him last week in Northampton." "Ah well" said John "he should know. But next time you come, bring the engine and let me have a look at it." I did so, and a few weeks later he returned the engine to me with scale-sized bogies – which did not foul the cylinders, and the engine not only ran without trouble for twenty years after that, but most of the rest of my engines went through the same process, being fitted with near-scale bogies built with centralising springs to bring the head of the engine round into a curve.

The job Bassett-Lowke said could not be done. Bassett-Lowke tinplate Flying Scotsman, *re-wheeled with flanged centre driving wheels and scale-sized bogies – by John Hart.*

Perhaps the most memorable instance of John's response to a challenge was a few years later, following a session on his railway in Surbiton. I had been working Polehampton at the far end of the garden, and in the gathering dusk a train of green Southern Railway coaches came towards me hauled by a 'King Arthur'. It was impressive, to say the least, and over supper I commented how realistic that train had looked, adding for good measure ''I wonder what that train would look like on a decent layout?'' John said nothing, but that moustache twitched. A few weeks later came the official opening of the newly built Ravensmoor terminus on the Crewchester line, attended by a full complement from both railway clubs. After the ceremony and luncheon, I was dismantling the PA system when Keith Andrews, one of John's young men, came up to me and said ''John would like you to come to Ravensmoor.'' Wondering what had gone wrong, I made my way to the covered terminus, where John and some of the boys were standing. John asked me to wait a moment as a train had been offered and was on its way, and even as he spoke, from the mouth of High Moor tunnel came – the King Arthur

Another job they said could not be done! 6ft 9in drivers on a Bassett-Lowke *Duchess of Montrose, fitted by Bob Lovell, by skimming down the flanges on the centre pair of drivers to about 0.5mm! John Hart added smoke-deflectors and double chimney, as well as building a new bogie assembly.*

and a set of green Southern Railway coaches! My railwaay was clockwork; John's was 12 volts third rail! The train made its way slowly into the main arrival platform, one of the Surbiton boys reached out to do something to the cab of the engine, and the train came to a halt. ''We thought you'd like to see that train on a 'decent' layout!'' said John. The laugh was well and truly on me, and it was not until much later that I found out just how it had been done. Each one of the Surbiton boys had secreted one coach in his lunch haversack, while John brought the engine. Behind that engine he had marshalled a utility van, packed with torch-batteries, and the engine had been fitted with a rheostat and switch.

By today's standards, John's model railway would be considered out-of-date, for not only was it coarse scale (as is Crewchester) but the outside-third rail tended to impart an old-fashioned appearance, as did the curves in the garage where Broadway station stood – the nerve-centre of the system. But closer inspection of his railway revealed his effective attempts to minimise the over-scale appearance of the track; for instance, where the emu ran between Westhaven and Broadway, the outside-third rail was of normal Gauge 0 bull-head rail, but out in the garden where trains were hauled by steam-outline or diesel locomotives only, the third rail was 00 section, thereby making it less obtrusive. Also, by using true scale-sized sleepers, placing them at true scale intervals, and using Bond's rail-chairs, which in those days were slightly smaller than other brands, much of the track was difficult to distinguish from fine-scale. Above all, the construction and maintenance of John's railway was of a high order, and so it withstood the punishing three-sessions-a-week which it was subjected to. Also, the fully interlocked colour-light signalling was not only based on prototype practice, but in one instance it superseded it, for it incorporated an approach lock release whereby if a train had been accepted into the section, and

the route setup, that route could not be altered until the train had passed over the section – an anti-panic measure. A signals inspector from nearby Esher on the Southern Region once visited John's railway, saw this device, and commented ''I could do with that on my line between Esher and Worcester Park!''

There is, however, a sinister side to this story, for I fear that, impressive as that approach lock release may have been, it was sadly abused when John was not present to see. If one of us had set up a wrong route, and then discovered our error, instead of going through the anti-panic routine of pressing the release button and then waiting for the two minutes to elapse before all tracks were returned to 'normal', someone would reach over to the master-switch and flick it off, thereby cutting off power to heating, lighting, and the entire railway system. The switch would then be thrown again to restore power and the approach lock release system by-passed!

IMPROVING THE BREED

If the year 1956 was a peak in the history of Crewchester, 1957 was a similarly dramatic year in my own business life, for I was invited to join the Education Department of Collins, publishers, of Glasgow, and so, after twelve extremely happy years with Novello's I moved from specialist music publishing to general educational work. My territory, which had spanned the entire British Isles, was now reduced to a slice of England which lay roughly east of a line drawn from Sheffield in the north, through London, and down to the western boundaries of Kent. This gave me more time at home, for I had less travelling to do, and my work was shared by five colleagues instead of having to play the lone wolf. Quite suddenly, school holidays became a reality, and whereas hitherto I had been obliged to attend all conferences and exhibitions wherever they may be held, now I was expected to attend only those on my 'patch'.

The model railway club thrived, and a smooth routine had settled upon weekends and holidays, although my duties as assistant organist at the local Parish Church did make further demands on my time; nevertheless, we did plan a further extension of the main line up the centre of the garden, releasing us from the bondage of a purely continuous circuit (see page 17) and giving us Ravensmoor and Inverblair stations. The double turnout on the north loop was built by John Blair, our first attempt at building our own points, and I might add in parenthesis that up to that time I had never even held a soldering iron in my hand!

The new extension was built on a gently rising gradient to reach Ravensmoor before continuing to a small terminus in the bottom right-hand corner of the garden named Inverblair, suggesting Scottish locale. This station was never more than a very temporary affair, was never developed, but did serve its purpose for a year or so while we planned a completely new layout. But Inverblair did provide the excuse to inaugurate a new named train called 'The Clansman', which ran non-stop from Inverblair to London. We already had one named train, 'The Crewcastrian', which ran between London, City Road, and Crewchester, and this run was well within the capabilities of any six-coupled clockwork mechanism. 'The Clansman', however did provide us with an operational problem brought about by that rising gradient, for the whole railway had been conceived and devised to be compatible with clockwork mechanisms. No mechanism could cope with a heavy train on a non-stop journey of 165ft, especially on an up-gradient, so once again we resorted to compromise.

'The Clansman' would normally be hauled by a Pacific, usually a 'Duchess' or 'Princess', and even on occasions by a 'Scot' (which had an identical mechanism). On the down run, the engine would be fully wound at London, would set off on its northward journey, running out of steam somewhere just north of Crewchester. At this point would occur a convenient signal check, giving the Crewchester operator time to re-wind the engine, after which it would tackle the gradient to Ravensmoor, and on to Inverblair. The up journey was slightly different, for much of the way lay on a falling gradient, and thus the train would probably run quite happily until it was within about twenty feet of its London destination. Once again, a fortuitous signal check allowed City Road operator to re-wind the engine so as to continue to City Road.

This might be a suitable point to answer the many questions put to me about how a clockwork system is operated, and to do this I must jump ahead in time a little to the new 1961 layout. How did we make trains stop at the required place? The answer is complex and devious! There were a number of cunning ploys, invariably unnoticed by casual spectators, and one of these involved the fact that Crewchester station was built on a slight plateau with the approaching tracks from each end rising an imperceptible ¼in in some ten feet. Therefore, a train approaching the station, and running out of steam, would have its speed checked by the rising gradient, the final check being imparted by the operator who would reach out his hand – not to the engine (which is where everyone was looking) – but to the last coach. A mere touch would impart a braking effect sufficient to cause the train to lose impetus and come to rest gently in the desired place. Knowledge and experience of the vagaries of every engine, coupled with long practice had brought this to a fine art! The engine would then be re-watered and would set off again, refreshed, the slight down-grade assisting departure.

At Ravensmoor terminus however a slightly different method was used in that the whole station lay in a sort of 'dish', dropping about ¼in, and rising towards the buffer stops, which were hydraulic. This device was highly effective, especially in the hands of an experienced operator who was familiar with all the vagaries of the different engines and their mechanisms. In the case of departures the dishing of the baseboard was even more effective. A train standing in the platform would be on the level, except for the last coach, which would be on that slight up-gradient towards the buffers, thus its weight was tending to want to push the train forward. The engine, fully wound, would be at the head of the train, rarin' to go, but a device at the rear of the train, operated from the trackside by bell-cranks, caused a rod to rise just in front of one of the rear axles of the last coach, preventing any movement. At the time for departure, all the Ravensmoor operator had to do was move a rod, the 'brake' would be removed from the train, and the engine would start, aided and abetted by that rear coach which was still on the down-grade slope. This completely foxed visitors, for they could never understand how that train

Rockhill Tunnel, looking north towards Crewchester.
August 1957.

started on its own!

Once under way, and on full wind, the engine would then encounter the compensating up-slope, thus inhibiting acceleration, so there would be no rocket-like departure from the station. One by one the coaches would reach the top of the slope, thereby lightening the load on the drawbar, and the train would begin to pick up speed. The principle was merely an adaptation of what the Central Line on the Underground used as common practice at every station! At City Road yet another device was used. Just before the line entered the garage, where the track was laid along the top of shelving and therefore dead level, there was a very slight 'hump' in the track, the effect of which was precisely similar to the humping and dishing already described.

But spring-drive produced enormous anomalies and inconsistencies, with engines of identical makes of mechanism performing in very different ways, so it took considerable experience to be able to despatch a given train with the engine correctly wound for its journey, having regard to the condition and type of mechanism, the engine itself (tank or tender), the weight and drag of the train itself, and even the weather-conditions. Very hot weather thinned the oil, while journals would expand within their bearings, all affecting running.

My step-son, David, did join in many of the running sessions, and indeed did qualify as supervisor, but he never quite developed the affection for railways which I did; his thoughts were more on aircraft, and in fact he did join the RAF when he left school. My younger son, Stuart, was far too small at this time to take any serious part in running the trains, although he evinced more natural interest in them than his elder brother. In due course he and his school friends became expert on the railway, but Stuart really started from where I had finished; his interest became far wider in transport as a whole, he collected a huge library of books on all aspects of transport, including railways, both steam and diesel, so that nowadays, if I want to look up a reference, it is to his library I usually have to resort. He is also a pillar of the local

Transport Society, and still occasionally joins in running sessions on the railway – a happy state of affairs.

The Easter Central Hall exhibition provided a meeting place for enthusiasts, although the national press seemed reluctant to recognise it for what it really was – meeting place where model engineers and enthusiasts may gather to see what was being done in the model world. Yet every year without fail, the news reporters would show hordes of children queueing at Central Hall, and add the gratuitous and wholly irrelevant comment ''. . . and there were quite a number of grown men there too!'' as if it were the toy department at a London store. But here I must confess that not all those 'grown men' acted entirely in character.

Norman Eagles and I were spending the time of day together there during a comparatively slack period, and we strolled up to a very fine Gauge One layout, comprising a terminus and track disappearing into what is usually referred to as a hidden 'fiddle-yard'. Norman was obviously well-known to the operators, who happened to be standing by, awaiting the time for the next demonstration. Beckoning me to follow him, Norman disappeared behind the curtain of the fiddle-yard, produced a small clockwork tank engine, and set it down on the stud-contact track. He then reached for the block-bell tapper and belled through 'light engine'. Startled operators the other end, after some hesitation, accepted the offer, and Norman belled through 'Train in section' which was also acknowledged. The engine, which, memory suggests was a Walker Fenn controlled speed loco, started its stately way out on to the main line. We dodged out to join the one or two spectators who were present, and watched the operators at the terminus frantically twisting their controllers in an effort to slow the approaching engine down, but it came on relentlessly, ignoring adverse signals and controller alike, until it ended up with a slight bump at the hydraulic buffers. Having realised what had happened, one of the operators turned and called out ''I'll bet that's (adjectival) Eagles! Where is he?'' But Norman was nowhere to be seen, being swallowed up in the crowd.

It was also at this time (1956) that the BBC came to make a short feature film on Crewchester, designed to last two minutes, and it took their cameraman all day to get those two minutes – something I now understand much better now I have ventured into the world of video. As I possessed no TV of my own in those days, I was able to see the result only on a friend's set.

There is another warmly-remembered character from this period, a friend named Basil Pumfrey, a Wodehouseian name which was greatly enhanced by his appearance, for he did bear a striking resemblance to some interpretations of Bertie Wooster. Unlike Wooster, however, Basil was possessed of a keen mind and brain, coupled with exceptional skills in improvisation. Added to all this, he was one of the kindest men I ever met, more often than not helping other people out at the expense of urgent work needed on his own house. Basil it was who suggested fine flint chick-grit as ballast on my railway, Basil who found for me builder's planks and oak uprights and baseboards when these were all but unobtainable and Basil who taught me how to soft-solder. When the car-port was built on to my house, Basil did the drawings and got planning permission; the same when I built an extension to the house – I had no architect's fee (Basil was qualified) for he did the drawings without a fee – ''Helps me keep my hand in, dear boy!'' If ever I was stuck for some hard-to-obtain item, Basil knew just where to find it. He died of that cruel scourge of humanity on his fifty-eighth birthday, but he is part of the Crewchester Railway, and never lost interest in it right up to the day he died.

The four-track main line between Rockhill and Crewchester Junction. August 1967 Bassett-Lowke A3 Windsor Lad *on down express.*

All my life I have been surrounded by the Basil Pumfreys of this world; so much so that it caused John Hart to observe one day "I never met a chap like you. Whatever your problem, whatever your need, the moment it happens, the one person who can solve it suddenly pops up out of the pavement in front of you. If you fell into the river, you would come out dry, with a trout in each pocket!" There is much truth in this accusation!

I continued my visits to Gainsborough where, once again I was able to acquire a second Bassett-Lowke A3, this time *Windsor Lad*, the first of the banjo-dome, long-lap valves and high-pressure boiler variety. I took it to show John Hart, who asked me if I realised that the valve-covers on the engine were wrong? I had not, and that led not only to my replacing the old valve-covers with correct ones, but largely modifying both *Flying Scotsman* (back to right-hand drive) and *Windsor Lad*, adding much detail such as reversing rods, wash-out plugs, and improved splashers over the driving wheels.

Our first scratch-built engine was not, however, that A2 made by George Hinchcliffe, but a Tilbury Tank built for us by a Suffolk farmer named Frank Friend, using a standard Bassett-Lowke 4-coupled mechanism, and that engine, now converted to 2-rail, still runs on Crewchester metals. It was through Frank that I first met Walter ('Wally') Mayhew, now recognised as being one of the finest Gauge O model makers of his time, but who, at the time I first met him, was working in 00 gauge. Johnny Watts, my erstwhile neighbour from Kelvedon days, kept in touch and even

made some station buildings for us, including a signal box which, thirty-eight years afterwards is still standing out in the garden, summer and winter.

With prices as they are today, it is interesting to reflect that a visit to Hattons shop in Smithdown Road, Liverpool, would secure Exley coaches at £1.50 each, or £1.75 with cast iron Mansell pattern wheels.

And so the 1950s rolled on, with the Crewchester Model Railway Club operating whenever possible, weather being the principal hazard, and the social side of the club growing year by year in importance. The annual Christmas Eve football match came into being, a suggestion made by one of the young members, followed by liberal refreshments back at the house, and in those days it was easy to muster two teams for the event. And then, in 1961, another milestone was passed.

Various flaws in the design and building of the railway were becoming so irritating that we had to consider drastic action. That line up the centre of the garden had rendered much of the railway inaccessible for purposes of maintenance, and there were one or two gaps between baseboard sections which were making the progress of the trains uncertain and dangerous. Worst of all, that central section, unlike the main line, had been built up on ash uprights instead of oak, and they were quickly rotting at the ground level. One Sunday in May 1961, while John Blair was staying with us, we came in from the garden, somewhat despondent about the state of things, and over lunch I said to John "You

26

know, one swift kick, and the whole lot would come down." My wife's comment was "Well, why don't you go and kick it!" To this day, I try to impute the highest of motives beind that remark, but the result was that after lunch we went out and administered such a kick as would commit us to major rebuilding.

For the whole of my summer holiday I worked at dismantling the entire railway, stacking baseboard for re-use, and returning track to component parts. One of the worst drawbacks to that layout had been the necessity to keep ducking backwards and forwards under the baseboard in order to work the trains, and even when one is young and fit, that can lose much of its charm when indulged to excess. Again we embarked upon a long period of planning, resulting in the decision to widen the entire baseboard sufficiently to build a four-track end-to-end main line, with a branch coming up the middle of the garden. This would mean no more ducking under baseboards; all track would be accessible for maintenance, and an intensive train service would be possible, for with four tracks, slow passenger and freight trains need not impede express traffic. The system chosen was that adopted by the LNER with fast roads in the centre, flanked by slow roads on each side.

But here again I must digress, for another project of that period came to an ignominious end; yet it is worth reporting for it illustrates how easy it is for enthusiasts to be carried away by their keenness without full investigation into the practicalities of the matter. The Walker Fenn controlled speed mechanism was no longer in production, but it was a highly effective, if somewhat over-scale affair, with a spring like a gramophone motor, and a well-made three-bob speed governor. Given half a chance, those engines would climb a brick wall, but if a spring did break, there was a very real risk of a broken thumb, for the winding arbor was a direct, rather than a geared wind. But there had come on to the market the Walker-Riemsdijk tank engine, a neat little job designed by John van Riemsdijk, and marketed by Walkers and Holtzappfel in two versions; the standard and the gradient models. Speed control was by means of a milled wheel which projected slightly from the cab top, and worked a delicate two-arm governor. Not as powerful as the Walker Fenn, but more to scale, this engine did not prove as popular as it ought to have done, such was the decline in interest in Gauge 0 at the time.

Fired with missionary zeal, I contacted John van Riemsdijk with a view to doing a sort of feasibility study, via the Guild and other model railway magazines, to try to resuscitate interest in the idea of a controlled-speed locomotive. Other manufacturers were marketing so-called controlled speed mechanisms, the best of which was Bassett-Lowke, but even that relied on a friction pad working on a brass wheel to reduce speed, thus imparting a braking effect. In due course a notice appeared in all model railway magazines, including the *Model Engineer*, asking for opinions on what would be the most popular type of controlled speed engine. On all sides I was assured that I would sell thousands; so, encouraged by this, I met John van Riemsdijk to discuss ways and means. Eventually the consensus was for a six-coupled mechanism rather than a complete locomotive, so that people could fit it to their own chosen engine. John had worked out that to provide tools, broaches, etc. for the job would mean an outlay of a large sum of money, even using the ones he already had, and that to break even, we must sell at least 2000 in the first year.

We waited for the orders to roll in, and the forecast of "You'll sell thousands, old man!" proved to be just a trifle optimistic. The total number of orders received was – twenty-two! So that was the end of that.

More successful was the saga of the so-called 'Teleguv', the name I bestowed on a somewhat revolutionary device which, during the 1960s, not only affected the Crewchester Railway, but a great number of other spring-driven layouts throughout the country.

The story has its beginnings in 1957, the year after the Gauge 0 Guild was formed. I received a letter from a Mr Fleming of south London, telling me of an idea thought up by a friend of his, an elderly gentleman by the name of Parr. It would appear that Mr Parr, a clockwork enthusiast, had been making a telephone call one day and while idly watching the dial run back to zero after each digit had been dialled, wondered how such a smooth movement was obtained; why did the dial not just fly back on a spring? Obtaining one of these telephone dials, he found inside a neat little two-bob governor which produced that gentle return-movement. Immediately, he began to consider whether it might be possible to introduce such a governor into the gear-train of a clockwork mechanism; so, taking a Bassett-Lowke standard 4-coupled mechanism, he built a bracket along the top, securing it to the side-frames, whereby the star-wheel of the mechanism engaged in the worm of the governor spindle. It worked!

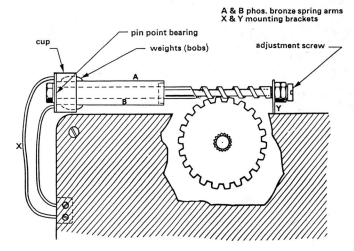

The 'teleguv' mounted on the frame of a clockwork mechanism.

Unlike all other speed speed-controls on commercially produced clockwork mechanisms, this did not rely on a friction-wheel or pad, but worked correctly, as a governor should, inhibiting the speed without inducing a braking effect, at that same time smoothing the flow of energy from the spring to the wheels. He also added a refinement of a sliding collar, controlled from the cab of the engine, which ran along the length of the leaf-springs holding the governor-bobs, thus forming a speed variation by compressing or releasing the centrifugal throw of the bobs.

Mr Parr showed the idea to Mr Fleming, who saw in it great potential if it could be marketed, but neither of these gentlemen wished to become involved in any commercial activities, but wondered if the Guild might be interested. I met Fleming at the Great Eastern Hotel at Liverpool Street in 1957, where he showed me the prototype 4-coupled mechanism fitted with the new telephone governor. The Guild, for legal reasons, were not in a position to enter any trading activities, so the mechanism was handed over to me, as a clockwork enthusiast, to do with as I

The author with Bob Lovell at Bob's home in Salisbury, 1969.

wished. I did approach Bassett-Lowke, but they were contemplating the abandonment of clockwork locomotives and were obviously not prepared to finance such a venture, and that original mechanism found its way into the body of an old Bassett-Lowke 4-4-0 which I had, and ran like that for years – and in fact is still running well on the garden railway of David East in Essex.

During the early 1960s I fell in with a young engineer named Bob Lovell, of Salisbury, who was exceedingly skilful in repairing and modifying clockwork mechanisms, and who had already done a first-rate repair job on an 0-6-0T for me. Bob came to Ipswich one day and saw the 4-4-0 running with its teleguv mechanism, was intrigued, and suggested that we ought to exploit this ingenious idea. After a period of experimenting, he came up with a version of the teleguv which could be adapted to any type of clockwork locomotive, be it slow goods or express passenger. His theory was that for any speed, that governor was far superior to the normal types found in commercial clockwork mechanisms in that it did not in any way impede the energy of the spring. Proof of this was a demonstration at Keen House before an audience of a hundred Gauge 0 Guild members, where he ran my Black Five on the test track until it came to a stand. He then lifted the engine from the track and the wheels revolved slowly through no more than two complete revolutions! This proved beyond all reasonable doubt that the full power of the spring was being utilised.

But the expertise of this young man went even further, for he had re-bushed all journals in that mechanism with phosphor-bronze and checked every gear for dead-true running. He then went on to astound his audience by marshalling a train of coaches which was so long that the rear coach was not far in front of the engine on that oval layout. Winding the engine fully, he set it in motion, and memory suggests that there were twenty-six bogie coaches behind that Black Five. The onlookers were not only astonished, but frankly incredulous, and, knowing that the track was wired for 2-rail electric conduction, demanded proof that they were not being hoodwinked. Once again, when the train came to rest, the engine was lifted from the track, and the wheels slowly revolved some half-dozen turns. The answer, as Bob explained to a still stunned audience, was that every one of those coaches had been fitted with PTFE bushes in the axle-boxes, and every journal had been made of silver steel and turned down to 0.040in diameter and highly burnished. This had the effect of reducing frictional resistance in the axle-box to an immeasurable minimum; in fact, if one stood a coach so fitted on a table, the chances are it would roll off, for the slightest gradient would allow it to roll. Derek Lucas,

another clockwork operator, had also had his engines and coaches treated by Bob, and they, too, were demonstrated at that meeting in Keen House.

So impressive was this break-through in one of the biggest problems in spring-drive, that I discussed with Bob the possibility of the entire Crewchester stud and coaching stock being put through his workshop, and thus began what was quite the most dramatic revolution in the running of the railway in its entire spring-driven history.

Although it means anticipating events at this stage, for we are still talking about the 1960s, it would appear logical to show just what this momentous development led to during the 1970s. The motley assembly of locomotives and rolling stock collected to run at Crewchester contained wheels of every profile, size, and back-to-back dimensions, which led John Hart to comment one day "Until you standardise on your wheels, you will be unable to standardise the settings of the check-rails and wing-rails on your points, and until you do that you cannot really hope to get reliable running through your turnouts." With nearly one hundred items of bogie stock and getting on for fifty engines I could not see anyone being prepared to undertake that huge job, especially someone like John who depended upon his modelling for his income. I certainly could not afford to put the work out to a professional engineer, but the idea of all stock having a standard profile and dimensions was an alluring one. Quite a few of our engines went to Bob Lovell for this 'teleguv' conversion, at which time he would fit PTFE bearings to tender wheels, and re-profile them to a properly coned shape with 28mm 'back to back' measurements. It was not until the early 1970s that Bob offered to go through the entire Crewchester stock, coaches, locomotives and bogie vans (4-wheeled wagons were already fitted with Jackson 28mm b-b wheels).

So began a period of some four years during which, every few months I would drive from Ipswich to Salisbury with a further batch of engines and a box of bogies, returning with a freshly turned wheels and a few 'teleguvved' engines. This period posed the operating superintendent at Crewchester considerable problems in loco allocation, for the balance between LNER and LMS motive power was often seriously disturbed, and it was only due to an amicable arrangement between the two companies that the trains were kept running. It became not uncommon to see an express of LNER teak stock running behind a Stanier Pacific, or an LNER A3 hauling a set of crimson lake stock. The most conspicuous result of all this was in the working of goods trains. Up to then, the procedure had been to prepare a goods train of four-wheeled stock, put an 0-6-0 freight engine at the front, offer it to Crewchester, set long-stop, silly-mid-off and deep extra cover(!), and then release the brake. Four-wheeled wagons were unsprung and travelling at speed are likely to detract substantially from the dignity of the railway in the event of derailment. But now, with the J39 and the J3 governed down to a mean speed of around 20mph, goods traffic could be despatched with every chance of its arriving safely at its destination. Local passenger trains too began to assume speeds more appropriate to their role, while the big Pacifics and 'Scots' ruled the roost with their 70mph trains lording it on the fast roads.

One cannot help wondering what might have happened to the whole scene of clockwork models had Mr Parr's invention come on to the scene twenty years earlier, but alas, this brilliant new star walked on to the stage just as the final curtain was coming down on the commercial production of clockwork engines.

4

BERNARD MILLER AND STANLEY NORRIS

Bestriding the history of model railways are giants such as Bassett-Lowke, Greenley, Keen, Stedman, and many others, some of them largely unsung; others which became household names, and to this Roll of Honour I would add the name of Stanley Norris, a man of great vision and ability who helped pave the way towards the standards of excellence we enjoy today. Before attempting to describe the man and his railway, however, the manner of our meeting might be worth re-telling.

I had first heard his name from J.N. Maskelyne, who had told me that it was not exactly the easiest thing to gain an invitation to visit his railway, and in fact Norris' own brother had never seen it! To receive such an invitation, said Maskelyne, was to have 'arrived' in the model railway world. It came as no surprise to me therefore to see an article in the *Model Railway News* (of which Maskelyne was the Editor) entitled "The Replanning and Rebuilding of Britain's Finest Layout – 0 Gauge at its Best". Although the article had been written by Norris, the title was by Maskelyne, and it has to be borne in mind that at the time this article was published fine-scale was comparatively rare, whereas today there are more Gauge 0 modellers working in fine than coarse scale.

At that time I am convinced that this model railway was unique, for I had never seen anything to surpass it, or indeed, equal it. Subsequently I had reason to revise this view, and of this, more later. I was all the more saddened, therefore, to see a letter published only a month after the appearance of that article in which a petulant writer denigrated the railway, pointing out that it was in no way representative of Gauge 0, and that "– anyone can do that sort of thing, given sufficient wealth." (Stanley Norris was a wealthy man). So incensed was I by this childish display of sour grapes that I wrote to the magazine deploring the attitude of the writer, pointing out that just because I ran a Morris car, that did not prevent me from admiring the beauty and perfection of a Rolls Royce; that we needs must know the best when we see it, and so on. Norris saw both letters and for me the results were far-reaching.

Not long before this, Norris had moved house from Black Gates, West Byfleet to an estate in Chilworth, known as Postford House, where he planned to build the railway featured in the *Model Railway News*. In this new layout he dispensed with all post-grouping stock, retaining only a mixture of LNWR, MR, LB&SCR, SE&CR, and a small amount of NER items. In this huge undertaking he was helped by Bernard Miller, probably one of the finest Gauge 0 Model builders of his generation, and who lived close by the new home of Stanley Norris. A long-standing friendship and personal association, coupled with a convenient financial arrangement made it possible for Norris to have first call upon Miller's services at almost any time, and here I would like to refute an allegation quite often heard in this connection – that Bernard Miller did all the work while Norris just sat back and paid him.

Nothing could be further from the truth, and is libellous to both men, for Norris was an accomplished modeller himself, and a considerable artist in his own right, as well as being an acknowledged authority of Italian Renaissance Art. I have seen models made by Norris when he was no more than twelve years old; workmanship which would do credit to a skilled man twice his age. It was Norris who built all the superb track for that railway.

John Hart had already become a regular visitor to Postford House by reason of Norris' interest in John's RM motors, which came about in this way. Among his locomotives Norris had a very small engine – possibly a Brighton 'Terrier' – for which he had found it impossible to obtain a reliable motor small enough to fit into the body, and compatible with his control system. On one visit he asked John if he could suggest a solution, and John, typically refusing to commit himself, took some measurements, went home and set to work to build a one-off motor specially for this job. As he remarked to me "You never know what this might lead to!" – his premonitions were later justified.

Taking the special RM motor on a subsequent visit, he tried out the motor, and after a touch here and there with a file it slipped in and the engine ran perfectly. So delighted was Norris with this that he commissioned John to fit his entire stud with the RM motor over a period of time, thereby necessitating a series of visits to Chilworth. It was on one of these visits, early in 1960 that Norris mentioned the correspondence in the *Model Railway News*, asking John if he had seen it. When John told him he had, and that Jack Ray was a friend of his, Norris immediately asked him if he would like to bring me over on one of his visits and spend an afternoon on the railway. So started a series of visits to Postford House for me, the first one being particularly memorable.

Bernard Miller and John Hart were already known to each other, each respecting the other's work, although John would always protest that he could never rank alongside Bernard as a model-maker. Be that as it may, both were highly thought of in the Gauge 0 world. A date was arranged, I drove to Surbiton, lunched with John and then went on to Chilworth, collecting Bernard Miller on the way. Arriving at the imposing gates, we passed through to where the drive divided, the left hand one going downwards into a dip in the ground where the house stood, and the right fork leading upwards to higher ground where a large shed had been built, 70ft by 22ft, containing the railway. Near to one end of this building was a door through which we entered, immediately being confronted by a double-track section mounted on a lifting bridge which was hospitably raised, and behind which stood Stanley Norris to greet us. Having done so, Norris invited me to wander round as I wished while he discussed some business with John.

The scene which met my eyes is difficult to describe without resorting to superlatives; the large shed with its sloping roof was illuminated by a network of fluorescent lights plus a row of

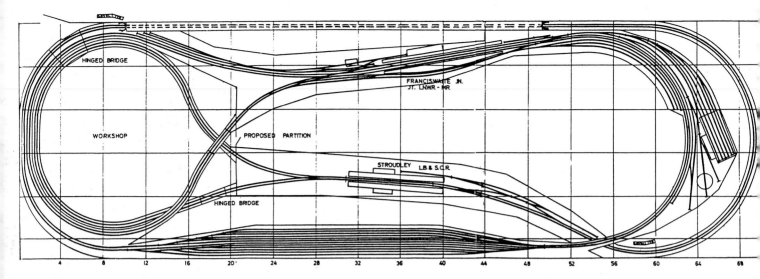

toplights which allowed daylight to penetrate. It was heated and air-conditioned, complete with humidifier, and at various points there were chairs, inviting the visitor to sit and obtain an eye-level view of the line; something I have always considered important, for model railways to be seen to best advantage they must be viewed from such an angle as would be normal when viewing the prototype. It was quite clear that there were certain positions on that vast layout which lent themselves to optimum viewing, and Norris had made full use of his artistic skills to obtain a convincing perspective. On subsequent visits he let me into some of his secrets. But on this first visit I was too overwhelmed to take in much more than an overall impression, and in something of a euphoric daze I tried to take in the complicated network of tracks, stations, tunnels, cutting and embankments.

The main features which struck me on first viewing were the extensive magazine of storage roads over by the far wall, under the toplights; next, the complex of Stroudley station with its junction, and then over at the far left end of the building the large engine sheds. To my left another junction merged at Franciswaite station, while the left hand wall sheltered a length of perfectly straight track, most of which was concealed in a tunnel. Norris did not like straight track, and in fact it was he who told me that there is nothing shortens the appearance of model track more than straight lengths. Apart from this concealed length – well over 50ft long, and the magazine – which was largely invisible from normal viewing positions, all track on the line was curved. The whole affair was a superb example of fine models running against a credible backdrop of scenery.

After half an hour of wandering from place to place, marvelling at everything I saw, I took one of the chairs and sat down so that I gained that true angle of perspective, and concentrated on a beautiful Midland Railway 4-4-0 with full inside working motion. With my head almost at track level I was drinking this all in when I felt a hand on my shoulder, and Norris stood behind me. "That, my boy, is the proper way to view a model railway." It was Norris – and it is many years since I have been addressed as "my boy"! John told me afterwards that the old man invariably followed this custom of inviting visitors to look round, while he would watch their reactions. If he thought they showed only superficial interest, they would not receive a second invitation – and indeed such people probably would not seek one – but if he perceived genuine interest, then one would be asked back, as I was, many times.

The track was a masterpiece of true scale bullhead, much of which had been laid by Norris himself, on a baseboard at table-top height, on a base of 3/8in blockboard on top of which went a layer of Dunlopillo carpet underlay, and over this a track-bed of 5mm ply. Not only did this eliminate the hollow drumming sound often produced by line laid direct on to ply, but it enabled him to adjust superelevation and levels by the mere turn of a screw. The wheel-beats over track joints was most convincing. Power for the locomotives was provided at 12v dc from high-capacity accumulators which delivered a far smoother flow of current and an almost unlimited supply of amps. Wheels were insulated at the rims with steel tyres shrunk on to them, thereby offering greater adhesion and eliminating wheel-slip.

At the time of Norris' death there were plans afoot to introduce full track-circuiting by superimposing an ac current over the dc, and the necessity for this was dramatically demonstrated during one of my later visits. Fortunately I was a mere spectator at the time, and not operating the trains! A train was standing in Francis-

Above:
The old (clockwork) 'race track'. No. 6113
CAMERONIAN heads a northbound express of the
newly-marketed LIMA coaches on the down fast line
between Rockhill and Crewchester Junction. For thirty
years this engine performed well on my railway and now
distinguishes herself on David East's ANDLEY-ON-SEA
garden railway in Dovercourt.

Below:
In the class-conscious Edwardian times you were
'somebody' if you travelled in the Pullman. Large boilered
Atlantic heads the Raven Pullman out of City Road,
passing the carriage maintenance sidings on the right and
the goods yard on the left.

Above:
End of the journey. Compound 1066 (one of three on the system) approaches the northern terminus of Ravensmoor with a semi-fast. This was the first true model of a known prototype ever to run on my railway.

Below:
The realisation of a lifetime's dream – to have a station which portrayed all the atmosphere of the busy terminus in a major city. The roof seems to echo to the bustle, the distorted announcements over indifferent P.A. systems, the clatter of porters' barrows, the sounds of escaping steam and the pant of Westinghouse pumps.

W.S. Norris' model of MR Johnson 2-4-0 No. 1478 approaches
Francisthwaite with a train of Clayton arc roof carriages.
(E.N. Corner Collection)

waite station, the engine having been uncoupled and run to sheds. I had been observing the procedure, carried out with the usual smooth movements, when my attention was diverted to my left where, coming round the long sweeping curve near the doorway came a train of LNWR stock hauled, if I remember correctly, by an 'Experiment' 4-6-0. I had no time to work out exactly which road was set for the oncoming express, but before I could draw Norris' attention to it the engine ploughed into the rear of the waiting Midland train in the platform, sending coaches over on their sides and bogies adrift from their vehicles lying all over the place. For a stunned moment I could not believe that this had happened on such a perfectly operated line, and Norris himself and Bernard Miller came quickly to the scene. Fortunately no permanent damage had been sustained, and everything was restored to normal within some ten minutes. It took ten minutes because all coaches were coupled by means of correct screw couplings which were the very devil to reach under the corridor gangways. Delicate tweezers were used, and once coupled, the weight had to be swung over until the tension was exactly sufficient to bring buffer-head to buffer-head. Thus, on curves, the inner buffers would be slightly compressed, so a uniform push-pull motion was maintained through the train. As Norris completed his task he muttered to me ''Goes to show that one should not operate a railway which is not fully signalled.'' Bernard whisphered into my ear ''Thank heaven I was not operating!''

Round about 4 o'clock, Stanley Norris would depart for the house, there to join his invalid wife for tea, leaving his visitors with a generous hamper-tea, for which Bernard would boil the kettle. Before departing for the house, Norris would select a non-fitted goods train from the magazine, set it going at about 20mph and then leave the track so pre-set that the train would run throughout the entire line, arriving back at the magazine. Known as 'the tea-time special goods' this train took *thirty minutes* to complete its journey! By the time the train was back at its starting point, Norris would be back.

Norris, as has been said, was an artist – a fact reflected in his scenery. He pointed out to me that the distant horizon, viewed

from train-level should never be more than five inches higher than the mean, even when distant mountains were involved. The effect of distance was greatly enhanced by the liberal use of purple hues, for, as he would point out, nature contains a great deal of purple. Then again, if one looked along a cutting, as at Stroudley where, with one's back to Francisaite, one of the lines beyond the double-junction ran away to the right, flanked by an embankment topped with conifers. These had been skilfully placed with slightly shorter trees as the line receded, again heightening the illusion of distance. Apart from relief building beside the track there were others painted on the backdrop; and any such building was always painted so as to present a 45° aspect, never square-on, and this minimised the unfortunate but unavoidable distortion of perspective which always happens unless one is dead-opposite the picture.

On another occasion, John Hart and I were up at the engine-sheds where we were admiring an LNWR locomotive, beautifully painted, lined out and lettered (few transfers were used on this railway – everything was hand-done). John commented that between the straw-coloured and red lining on the prototype there was in fact a thin line of yellow, only ¼in thick on the full-sized engine, and that, thin as it was, it imparted quite a different overall effect. Bernard was standing nearby, and agreed. On our next visit, John noticed that that same engine was standing in exactly the same position by the sheds, and something made him go up to examine it more closely. I saw him take out his pocket-lens and study the engine even more minutely. Then: ''Bernard, you old so-and-so – you've done it!'' To me he handed his lens – ''Here, Jack – just take a look at that!'' What I saw was a hair-line of yellow between the straw and red lining. John turned to Bernard, ''How on earth did you manage that?'' Bernard grinned. ''With a very powerful magnifying glass, a tiger's whisker, and shattered nerves.''

Stroudley 0-4-2 Carew D. Gilbert **heads a train of LB&SCR**
carriages through Stroudley on the Norris layout.
                                                    (E.N. Corner Collection)

On yet another occasion, Norris, having greeted us, confessed
that he was either not feeling too fit himself, or it might have been
his wife was unwell, but he asked us to excuse him, leaving us in
the care of Bernard Miller, whom, as usual we had brought with us.
Tea, as usual had been laid on. Now, it had been very noticeable on
all my visits that Norris never stopped a train in a station, unless, as
happened on that fateful occasion at Franciswaite, it was necessary
to change the engine. When I asked him why this was so he replied
"I am not really all that concerned with running a train service as
such, but rather to go out on a summer's day with a pack of sand-
wiches and a flask, find a good place to sit on some embankment,
and just watch the trains go by." So I had never seen trains come
into Stroudley and stop; but on this occasion Bernard was in
charge, so John asked him "Let's have some real train-movements,
Bernard, calling at these fine stations." And fine stations they were
too, with every course of bricks faithfully modelled, and even sash-
windows which could be raised or lowered by means of tweezers.
So for that afternoon the trains arrived and departed from the two
stations, and goods trains shunted in the yard at Stroudley, where
we saw one 35-wagon train propelled into the sidings and passing
over three sets of slips and turnouts without the faintest suggestion
of a judder at the frogs.

I have been privileged to watch Bernard Miller at work on a
model, from which it was clear to see why his locomotives were so
fine; he had monumental patience, considerable skill, and time
just did not exist for him. It is arguable that there have been better
modellers than Bernard, but it must be remembered that he was

one of the true pioneers of fine-scale, setting standards for others
to follow and even improve upon. I watched him at work on a GER
'Claud Hamilton' 4-4-0, for which he was making a driving wheel
splasher from nickel silver. To my untutored eyes, that sliver of
metal was just about perfect, but he worked away on it with his
needle file until he was able to drop it into position on the engine
where it sat happily even without solder – a perfect fit. He then
spent some ten minutes preparing and tinning his iron until it was
as he wanted it. Three tiny 'spot-welds' were performed and then
the iron was run along the joint slowly and steadily so that the
solder flowed like paint from an artist's brush. The finished job
seemed to me to be just about perfect, and Miller sat there
regarding it through his half-moon spectacles for some minutes,
grinned up at me and said "Yes – that is coming along quite
nicely". He then proceeded to heat the iron again, remove the
splasher, which he cleaned thoroughly, and then set to work on it
with fine emery! That engine was five years in the building. But
that was Bernard Miller, and at times his total disregard for time
could be rather inconvenient.

This was never better exemplified than on the day when I drove
George Hinchcliffe, and Walter Mayhew over to Postford House,
a long drive with a detour to take in Surbiton. This was in fact the
day when Norris was not able to stay with us during the afternoon
and towards the end of that session a train failed in that long
straight tunnel. Bernard's remedy was to send a light engine round
on to the rear of that train and literally thump it along with a series
of shunts backwards and forwards until the engine could be
reached. That engine was then taken to the workbench which lay
right opposite the entrance door of the railway room, and Bernard
sat down with the failed engine to discover the cause of the
trouble.

He had insisted that we visit his cottage for tea on the way home – a long cross-country drive with no motorways – his wife expecting us somewhere round about 5 o'clock. It was almost that time when he started work, and for almost an hour he sat there happily testing various circuitry, while we watched the clock move on towards 6 o'clock. We suggested that it would be better if we just dropped him at his cottage on the way home and went straight on, for it was a very long drive, and we would not be home until ten, even if we left immediately. But no – that engine had to be put right before he left the premises, and no – we must stay for tea; we were expected! Soon after six, the faulty collector had been located, removed, and replaced, and the engine tested before we left. Tea proved to be a protracted and leisurely affair despite our mentioning that we really had to make a start, but it all fell on deaf, ableit very friendly and hospitable ears. Somewhere about 8 o'clock we set sail over darkening countryside, steering a tortuous route for Ipswich. Now, George Hinchcliffe and I share a great love of Haydn's music, and he was sitting beside me in the front passenger's seat, 'Wally' Mayhew behind. We started a sort of mutual quiz, each singing (and I use the word in its broadest interpretation) snatches of the Haydn symphonies, and trying to floor the other. Neither of us had exactly a trained singing voice, and I think Wally Mayhew must remember that journey for the rest of his life!

The meeting of Walter Mayhew, Norris, and Miller was a case of deep calling to deep, for it altered Mayhew's entire modelling life thereafter. He saw his ideal medium, and within a year of that visit he had become very friendly with both Norris and Miller, staying at the house with Norris for weekends, and entertaining Miller in his own home. Eventually he took one of his first attempts in fine-scale 7mm down to show Norris. I cannot be too certain whether it was the Holden 4-6-0 or the huge *Cock o' the North*, but Norris walked round it examining it from end to end for some time and then observed ''It's as good as anything I've got. Too big – but a fine model.'' (Norris had disposed of all his big engines). It was the accolade.

This very inadequate account of the Norris railway, and the man is merely a glimpse of what, for me, was at that time undoubtedly Britain's Finest Layout, as Maskelyne had dubbed it. A letter I received from Stanley Norris shortly after Maskelyne's death in 1959 could well be applied to the writer in some considerable measure, and I quote it in full. It says much about the man.

1.6.60

Postford House
Chilworth, Surrey

Dear Mr Ray,

Thank you for your letter of 29th May. The afternoon of Thursday 16th June will suit me, and I will expect you, John Hart, and Bernard about 3 p.m. John is due here anyway in the near future, and may combine the visit.

Yes, I knew J.N.M. well, and for nearly thirty years. His death is a blow to me, not only because a great genius has passed away, but because I delighted in his company, and in his generous and tolerant nature. He was not only a great expert, but a great man.

It was he above all that held up the lamp of perfectionism. Without him the path will be more difficult. But we must keep on trying.

Yours sincerely
W. Stanley Norris

Norris died a few years later, and his dearest wish that the railway should go to Kensington Science Museum was never realised for there was neither the room nor the staff to maintain and operate it. Sadly, much of it was broken up and disposed of, but thanks to the efforts of Wally Mayhew and Arthur Dewar, some of it went to them, including the two stations and some of the rolling stock and engines. At least these are in safe hands.

It would be patently unfair to a number of people to leave the impression that there has been nothing better since Miller and Norris. Standards in modelling have improved out of all knowledge since those days, and there must be a number of model railways today which have indeed surpassed the high standards of the Norris railway. Names and comparisons can be invidious, but one stands out in my own mind – that of Neil Corner. Inspired by the work of Miller and Norris, and himself a fine engineer, Neil Corner has embarked upon a project in 7mm modelling which is quite breath-taking in its sheer audacity of design, extent, and in modelling standards. I have been privileged to visit this railway in its as yet incomplete form, but hope to see it again when it is in full running order. As with any such vast undertaking, many people are involved, all bringing their individual skills to the project, and I am quite sure that most of them would readily acknowledge their indebtedness to the example set by Miller and Norris. Thus is the torch those two men lit carried, lighting the way for others, and inspiring us to even higher peaks of accomplishment and excellence.

*Webb LNWR 'Cauliflower' 0-6-0 No. 25
passes the marshalling yard at the approach
to Francisthwaite.*   (E.N. Corner Collection)

5

THE 1960s & THE FOUR-TRACK MAIN LINE

The new four-track layout of the Crewchester Railway, started in 1961 had been planned in phases, each phase to be completed before going on to the next. This rule was relaxed to the extent that while the track was being ballasted and scenery added, lineside effects installed, &c., we would lay a temporary length of track beyond there just in order to be able to run trains. It is a good precept when building a model railway to get something running, otherwise it is possible to get so bogged down with plans and modifications that interest in the purpose of the railway can be lost. By the mid-1960s it was possible to run trains to the site of Ravensmoor, although it would be some time before the permanent station would be built.

The Crewchester Model Railway Club was now a thriving institution, and over the thirty-five years of its history it is interesting to look back and reflect on the different approaches by the boys to the railway. Steam, although on the wane on British Railways, was still very much with us, so schoolboys of thirteen upwards could identify with what they saw at Crewchester, even though few of them could remember pre-nationalisation. There were those who came along merely because a friend, or a brother was a member, mainly for the social aspect of the club, and most of these would gradually acquire some degree of enthusiasm for the hobby. Then there were those who had some type of model railway of their own, most likely in 00 Gauge, who were attracted to the greater scope and scale of Gauge 0, and who were keen to learn more of correct railway practice.

The 'creme-de-la-creme' were the one or two boys who appeared on the scene but rarely – perhaps only one in a few years; the type of boy who seemed to 'live' the railway. Such boys stood out apart from the crowd, for when they were operating it was quite clear that they were not seeing models at all; they were actually on the footplate, driving, or standing on the platform, watching real trains. Such empathy was indeed rare, but it was good to see, and it is noticeable that this elite handful of members has never completely lost touch with Crewchester, for it was an important part of their teen-age, impressionable years which will obviously remain with them for the rest of their lives. Yet all the boys who joined Crewchester had one thing in common; they were boys who would always make something of their lives – the kind who take up hobbies – described by educationalists as "the clubbable 10%" whatever that may mean! Many of them have gone on to highly successful careers and are obviously destined to reach the top of their profession. Quite a few have gone to the railways for their employment, usually in signalling; but whatever

degree of success they achieve, I am grateful to have been privileged to watch those formative years and possibly have had some tiny part in their growing up.

It might be worth pausing here for a while to consider a typical day's operating during those mid-1960s. On a Saturday morning, if the weather was fine, I would be out in the garage by 9am, preparing for the arrival of the boys. The log would be open and ready for signature; nests of keys, all labelled for the various operating positions would be laid out in the garage, and the statutory yellow duster for every operator made ready. This was to prevent perspiring fingers touching the paintwork of engines whilst winding. About 9.30am, bicycles would begin to arrive bearing the young members and after parking these machines, the boys would sign the log. Duty Officer for the day would be appointed from the ranks of supervisor, and he would then assume responsibility for appointing boys to their respective operating positions.

The next decision was just which method of track cleaning would be appropriate for that day, this being dictated by weather over the preceding week. Had it been a dry week, a mere rub over the track with a cloth slightly moistened with paraffin, followed by a wipe with a dry duster would be sufficient, but if there had been rain, fine emery-cloth would be used first, followed by a dry wipe. All wheels were kept highly polished by routine wheel-cleaning sessions, a practice which seemed to occasion much comment and even questions from visitors who imagined that for clockwork trains these things did not really matter. This was just not true, for the difference between running on dirty track and dirty wheels, and with clean track and wheels can be summarised thus: a Pacific engine would just about manage a five-car train from Ravensmoor to City Road (garage) on dirty track, but that same engine would haul nine coaches with ease over the same track when it was clean.

I am reminded of a visit from Frank Shaw, who used to write under the name of "Birkonian" in the model press, and was a keen clockwork operator, with a penchant for building very fine private-owner wagons. He stood at the back door of my garage one day watching one of the Bassett-Lowke compounds run down the garden with four heavy steel Exley coaches. He commended "You younger chaps have left us old 'uns behind, you know. Why can't I get running like that?" He produced a Bassett-Lowke compound of his own and we set it on the track with two coaches, where it struggled some forty feet and stopped. The reason was not far to seek, although I did not tell him so; it would have been unkind. The wheels of his engine had a tyre of mud some millimetre thick

The total locomotive stud assembled outside Crewchester Junction in 1962. Thirty three engines are on view of which just seven are not tender locomotives.

– bogies, drivers, and those terrible diecast tender-wheels – all were encrusted with years of dirt picked up from the track. I know now only too well how Frank Shaw felt when he spoke of the younger generation leaving the older ones behind, for I now find myself in precisely the same situation, with the new generation accomplishing feats of electrical engineering and operating far beyond my own skills or even understanding.

Having cleaned the track, the next duty was for each Senior Member (a definite rank in the hierarchy of Crewchester) at each station to collect from the storage cupboards in the garage their allocation of locomotives and take them to their position on the line. Meanwhile, under the direction of the Duty Officer the rolling stock, passenger and goods, would be moved to whatever place the timetable for the day dictated; the timetable was normally scheduled to start round about 10.30am. This was the time for what became known as "T'yup!" – a corruption of "Tea up!" when beakers of tea would be distributed to members. The timetable would then be started, usually finishing at 12.30pm, with an hour and a half for lunch, and then resumed at 2pm until 5.30pm. In high summer, sessions would often be continued from about 6pm until 8.30 or 9.00pm, when all trains would be run into City Road (the garage), the locomotives put away, wrapped in yellow dusters, and the coaches marshalled on the tracks inside the garage. A huge blackboard mounted on the door of the garage (it is still there today!) listed every one of the engines we possessed and every run would be logged on this board.

When everything had been put away, the Duty Officer with the help of a Senior Member would call over the number of trips made by every engine, these details being entered in the log so that we had a record of just how long springs lasted, and in which engines.

It also provided a very practical guide to engine allocation for any excessive use of one engine would show up conspicuously, and neglected engines would also be clearly seen. It was then 'goodnight', and a stream of cycles would pour out into the road; I would lock up and come indoors. They were strenuous and exciting days, and I could not possibly cope today with the sheer physical and mental labour involved in running the railway and the club. And, speaking of physical labour, remember that every engine had to be wound up for every trip!

There was also a Damoclean sword hanging above our heads – the possibility of a broken spring, or even worse, a stripped ratchet. Possessing no mechanical skill myself, I had to rely on Bob Lovell for ratchet repairs, but as this entailed a 300-mile return journey to Salisbury, it was as well that we were well stocked with engines to spare. Unless a train running from London to Ravensmoor was to do the return journey with the same engine, we needed a basic serviceable stud of 35 engines to run a timetable. While broken ratchets were beyond my scope to repair, there was something I could do about springs – and I did it – with far-reaching effects.

Towards the end of the 1950s, the writing began to appear on the wall. In short, one after another, the big names in Gauge 0 began to vanish from the scene: the Leeds Model Co., Mills Brothers, Bassett-Lowke, Walkers & Holtzappfel, leaving Bonds as the sole representative of a once-thriving industry, and had it not been for the appearance of the Gauge 0 Guild, the demise of Gauge 0 would have been a very real possibility. There was now no firm willing or able to supply springs, and clockwork enthusiasts had to rely on the second-hand market for their mechanisms and springs. In desperation, I made a trip to Sheffield to try to find a firm who would make springs for me, but, lacking any technical expertise myself, I was unable to prepare detailed specifications of the two main types, namely Bassett-Lowke 4 and 6 coupled mechanisms, so I took some sample springs with me. Eventually I discovered a small back-street firm called Invicta Springs, managed by a benevolent Mr Tingle, who immediately showed keen interest in my dilemma, especially as he had known Frank Mills of Mills Bros.

Mr Tingle offered to make up one or two examples of each type, which, if successful could be turned out as a batch. No deposit was asked, and I remember this kindly man with gratitude, for the business I could offer him was insignificant. I think it was possibly his acquaintance with Frank Mills which influenced his decision to be so helpful, for Mills Bros. had produced many models similar to ones for which I now sought springs. In due course I heard that my springs were ready, but even then Mr Tingle would take no money until I had tried the samples out. I immediately placed notices in the Guild Gazette and model press, inviting anyone who needed springs for Bassett-Lowke 4- or 6-coupled mechanisms to contact me, and the resultant orders made it possible for me to place quite a substantial bulk order with Invicta, as well as supplying a spring-thirsty community with much-needed nourishment. Periodically during the following twenty years, I organised similar exercises, with Derek Lucas taking over on one occasion when I was unable to. Unhappily, Invicta became swallowed up in the maw of the giant Firth-Brown, so that personal touch was lost. At this time Bob Lovell appeared on the scene and with his engineering expertise we were able to draw up detailed specifications of four types of spring so that I could widen my horizon. The whole thing was done on a non-profit-making basis, and never at any time did one single person let me down for payment – a remarkable tribute to the hobby!

Invicta having left the stage, I turned to Knights of Potters Bar, and quickly established a cordial relationship with their Directors, so that they were able to import Swedish steel and dress it specifically for our needs, and, incidentally, waiving their rigid rule of requiring a substantial deposit, provided I would undertake to settle the account in full within 28 days of completion. This gave me just a month to colour-code, sort, invoice, pack and despatch some £3000 worth of springs and recover the money – an anxious period. It was a considerable undertaking, involving several journeys from Ipswich to Potters Bar during the production of the springs, and the last time I undertook this task was 1979 when the total value of springs ordered exceeded £3500. Clockwork, it would appear, was far from dead. Some of the letters I received from people who had bought these springs were quite moving, like the Parson in Devon whose pre-war layout had lain dormant for twenty years, all the engines having broken or worn out their springs, but now, to the great delight of his grand-children, it was once again in full service.

It was during this time that I first came into contact with Drew Donaldson, whose amazing system of Irish Railways was run exclusively on clockwork. Where most orders I received were for up to six or seven, Drew would order fifty or more. As the minimum order for any one type of spring was 200 – less than this would have made the venture uneconomic – Drew's order was often just the difference between being able to place that minimum order or not. Altogether, over the years I suppose I must have supplied well over 5000 springs, and this brought me many new friends. Even today, some twelve years after my last spring-supplying exercise, I still receive echoes of the scheme, with someone ringing up to ask if I was still able to supply.

Most people at some time of their lives encounter some trivial incident which has the most widespread and dramatic repercussions, and the 1960s brought me one such. I had been to lunch with the Headmaster of a new Secondary school in the remote Norfolk village of Reepham, and had spent most of the afternoon

Tom Dack
Headmaster, Reepham
Primary School, Norfolk.

1968. The NER 4-6-0 Class S
from Rev. Parley's collection,
approaches Crewchester
Junction with an empty
coaching stock train.

with him. Leaving the school about half past three, I made my way towards my hotel in Holt, and, while passing through the village, spotted a tiny country primary school. Normally, I would not call upon such a school, for there would be at the most, two teachers, both taking classes. However, I decided on the spur of the moment to look in and pay a courtesy call and if possible, have a word with the Head, only to discover that it was just a two-teacher school where the Head was teaching all day. In this case, the Headmaster turned out to be a Mr Tom Dack who entertained me in the classroom where he was teaching, and for a few minutes we chatted, while a class of very well-behaved 10-11 year olds, obviously accustomed to having visitors to their classroom, showed no more than passing interest in my intrusion. Tom Dack was a Norfolkman, born and bred, with a touch of attractive brogue in his speech, and reacted positively when I mentioned that I had been down to explore the railway stations (two) in the village, or at least, what was left of them.

"You interested in railways, then?" Tom asked me, and when I brought out one or two photographs of Crewchester he immediately dismissed his class – fifteen minutes before time – and said "You'd better stop to tea." I was led out of the school building, across the yard, in through a gate in the wall of the school-house garden, and into the garden. On our right was a large shed, which Tom Dack proceeded to unlock. Inside was a series of Gauge 0 tracks running right round the shed, dotted with all kinds of locomotives and rolling stock whose provenance I could not even guess at. Among these were one or two recognisable commercial models such as the ubiquitous *George the Fifth* and *Duke of York*, but other, rather over-scale engines were also seen.

Tom explained that his son had no interest in the railway, and his principal recreation these days was sailing, he and his daughter taking practically all the available pennants on the Norfolk coast! He told me he wanted to sell all this stuff but could not be bothered to go in for all the advertising and hassle of having lists prepared and distributed. Then quite an astonishing thing happened. He dragged from under the baseboard a huge chest from which he began to extract a series of model locomotives such as I had never seen before; all of GNR or NER pattern, all slightly over-scale, but all quite clearly recognisable from their prototypes. And all clockwork. As the engines were put, one by one, on to the track, I suddenly realised what they were – surely this must be the stud of engines built by Rev Parley, Arthur Dewar's old friend, of Tivetshall St Mary, Norfolk!

"Where on earth did you get these from?" I asked my host.

"Oh, I bought these as a job lot from an old Norfolk parson, chap named Parley. He died about 1956, and anyway was getting too arthritic to run his railway – went all round his kitchen-garden, it did!" Then he added "You interested?"

Interested? I was speechless – both at the sight of these models, crude as some of them were, but also the coincidence of that chance visit to a school I would normally never have gone to, absolutely on impulse, and suddenly solving the mystery of just what had happened to Parley's engines. What followed would take a long time to tell, but briefly, I undertook to make an inventory of all items, value them, and insert adverts in the model press, Tom to

The goods yard at Ravensmoor: the Rev. Parley's J3 marshals a freight train.

Two angles on the same scene; the N.E.R. Class Q 4-4-0 at High Moor with a down stopping passenger train for Ravensmoor.

reimburse me if and when sales transpired. But he did give me first refusal of some of the more interesting Parley engines, such as the NER Class S 4-6-0, two NER Class M 4-4-0s, a Q1 ("Railcrusher"), GNR J3 and several other items. So glad was he to be relieved of the task of advertising that he put a ridiculously low figure of the engines I chose. One may well imagine Arthur Dewar's surprise and delight when I told him what had happened.

But there was a sequel to all this quite some years later which may be told now. Both the BBC and ITV had made programmes – very short in duration – on Crewchester, one of which had been followed in the same week by an article on my railway which appeared in the East Anglian Daily Times, together with photographs which included one or two of the recently-acquired Parley engines. Shortly after this, on a blazing hot July day, with the temperature well up into the nineties, we were running an 'open day' for visitors, which had also been advertised. About two o'clock there appeared at the top of my garden a very aged couple, the man walking with the aid of a stick, and I went to greet them. In the very broadest of Norfolk brogues, the man told me "Oi hup yew dun moind us a-coming along, but we see that programme on the TV and then the pictures in th' paper; Oi say ter my mussus, Oi say, 'Thass Mr Parley's injuns, that is. We're a-goin' t' git to Ipswich and see them agin if that can be done.' So we gits the bus from the main rud, an' then the trolley t' Rushmere Heath and here we are."

I hastened to fetch two chairs for this wonderful old couple, who must have been well into their eighties, plied them with cups of tea, while the man poured out his story of how in his younger days he would go round the Tivetshall Rectory to work Mr Parley's model railway. Many a time, he told me, he had wound those engines and sent them on their way during the 1930s. So, one by one I ran those engines to where he could handle them, although his arthritic hands could no longer manage the winding. But his delight in seeing the locomotives was marvellous to see, his wife obviously sharing his pleasure. It was a daunting journey they had undertaken, especially on such a blistering day, and I was greatly touched that such lasting affection for those models had led to making the trip. Later, I drove them into Ipswich to catch the Norfolk bus, and never heard of them again. Only one of those engines remains with me today – the J3 0-6-0, and is a reminder of those bygone days.

Meanwhile, life continued at Crewchester, and, bit by bit the line crept northwards until the time had come to undertake the most ambitious project ever – a large covered terminus with freight yards, carriage sidings, and MPD with turntable. Crewchester Junction station had been completed, but as yet lacked the branch line up the Vale of Trenton, thereby justifying the inclusion of 'Junction' in the station's name. A bay had been provided on the down (west) side of the station to accommodate the branch-line push-pull train, and the five through platforms had been put into service. North of the station the four tracks ran into a cutting before plunging into High Moor tunnel, and it was north of this tunnel that the fun really began!

It had long been my ambition to have a really large terminus with covered roof and with all the atmosphere of bustle associated with such a station. During 1964 I started to build the baseboard for this project, almost scaring myself to death in the process, for when I saw the bare expanse of baseboard I really thought it looked like nothing so much as the stage of the London Palladium! In the event there was barely room to squeeze in the requisite points to give access to and from every running route to every platform. It contained six platforms of various lengths, from nearly 18ft down to a mere 10ft, with a bay between the arrival and departure sides. In between platforms 2 and 3 a carriage siding was laid, offering accommodation for the longest conceivable train, while on the arrival side, between platforms 4 and 5, lay a similar sidings, thus solving the problem of space for empty stock. Colonel Vaux very kindly made us some wooden rafters to support the roof, which was glass, the whole thing supported by high wooden pillars. This showed a distinct tendency to sway somewhat in a high wind, so a weather-screen was fitted on to the country end of the overall roof, earning it the uncomplimentary description of "the bedstead roof." It had two disadvantages; the roof did not span the entire station, and the pillars tended to obscure the view along the station from the circulating area. However, it served us well for a few years while plans were drawn up for a Barlow-style overall roof similar to St Pancras.

Operation at Ravensmoor was interesting. Main line trains would come into platforms 4, 5 or 6, but No. 6 was the only one with relief points to allow an engine to run round, consequently it was used principally by suburban trains with tank locomotives. The main arrival platform was No. 4, being not only the longest on the arrival side, but offering no deflection from the down main line. The bay between arrival and departure sides were used for the occasional excursion train, but more often for parcels vans, and the sleeping cars from the night trains. The first arrival of the morning was an unusually long LMS train, sometimes double-headed by a Pacific and a compound, carrying sleeping accommodation. The sleeping car would be shunted to the bay so that passengers could alight at leisure, after which it would be taken to the buffer-stops at the far end of the Departure storage road between platforms 2 and 3 to await the up night train, which was usually the last up movement of the day. A train, having arrived at Ravensmoor, after passengers had alighted, would be taken by the pilot out of the station and then backed into the departure side, either at a platform, or if not due to leave for some time, on to the carriage storage road. The engine would then run to sheds to be serviced, turned and prepared for its next turn of duty. We did try to avoid an engine taking out the same train it had brought in.

One very serious but unavoidable flaw in the layout of Ravensmoor was the necessity to move arriving freight trains right across the throat of the station in order to reach the goods reception road alongside platform 1. This would of course have been unthinkable in full-size practice, but the exigencies of space dictated the procedure. On the outskirts of Ravensmoor lay the suburb of High Moor where a station had been built, served only by the two slow roads; no main line trains called here, nor were there any goods facilities. It was purely a passenger station which relieved to some extent the pressure on the main line station, rather as York Road did for King's Cross.

We had acquired, through the PRO British Railways (as they were then called) a large crate of block instruments, including tapper-keys and bells, three-position single-pegger instruments, and repeater instruments. Now Ravensmoor was operational, plans were put into effect to install these, with three main block posts, City Road, Crewchester Junction and Ravensmoor. There is something immensely satisfying in offering and accepting trains by means of the identical telegraph instruments used on to the railway. To celebrate the inauguration of these instruments we had a visit from John Hart and his band of boys from Surbiton, who took part in the first session on Sunday 29th August 1965. The idea had been to eliminate the objectionable practice of shouting up and down the garden things like "Can you accept an express passenger train?" to which the answer might be "Not yet – I haven't a spare platform" etc, which was not only annoying to neighbours but far from correct practice. When the twelve block bells and instruments had been installed and were working during a hectic train service I am not too sure whether the neighbours might have preferred the shouting!

Life was not entirely a 7mm affair during that decade, for I visited several narrow gauge lines, becoming a member of the Ravenglass and Eskdale Railway, where Doug Fereira gave me footplate passes on both the *River Esk* and the *River Irt*. I was also taken by George Hinchcliffe and Arthur Dewar to Stapleford Park, where I was introduced to John Gretton and David Garnock. John Gretton, who later succeeded to his fathers' title, not only acted as our host, but when 6 o'clock came and the general public departed, gave us one of the trains, headed by one his beautiful

Members of the Crewchester Model Railway Club operating at Crewchester.

E.A.D.T.

The author with young Michael Read at Ravensmoor during a session in 1967. E.A.D.T.

Atlantic engines, to run up and down between the main station and Lakeside, taking it in turns to drive. It was not until we were on our way home that Arthur told me that my affable companion that afternoon was Viscount Garnock, owner of the Gresley K4 *The Great Marquess*. It was rather typical of John Gretton that when we were playing trains with his own railway, and some late visitors, not realising that the place was now officially closed asked if they could board the train, he asked us if we minded!

The first Ravensmoor Queen Street terminus.

4472 Flying Scotsman *approaches Ravensmoor with a Down express.*

The block instruments at Crewchester Junction, being operated by young John Howard, now Dr. Howard.

Hornby D49 The Bramham Moor *leaves Ravensmoor platform 6 with an up local train for Crewchester Junction. Engine re-wheeled, Lentz rotary cam valve gear fitted by John Hart.*

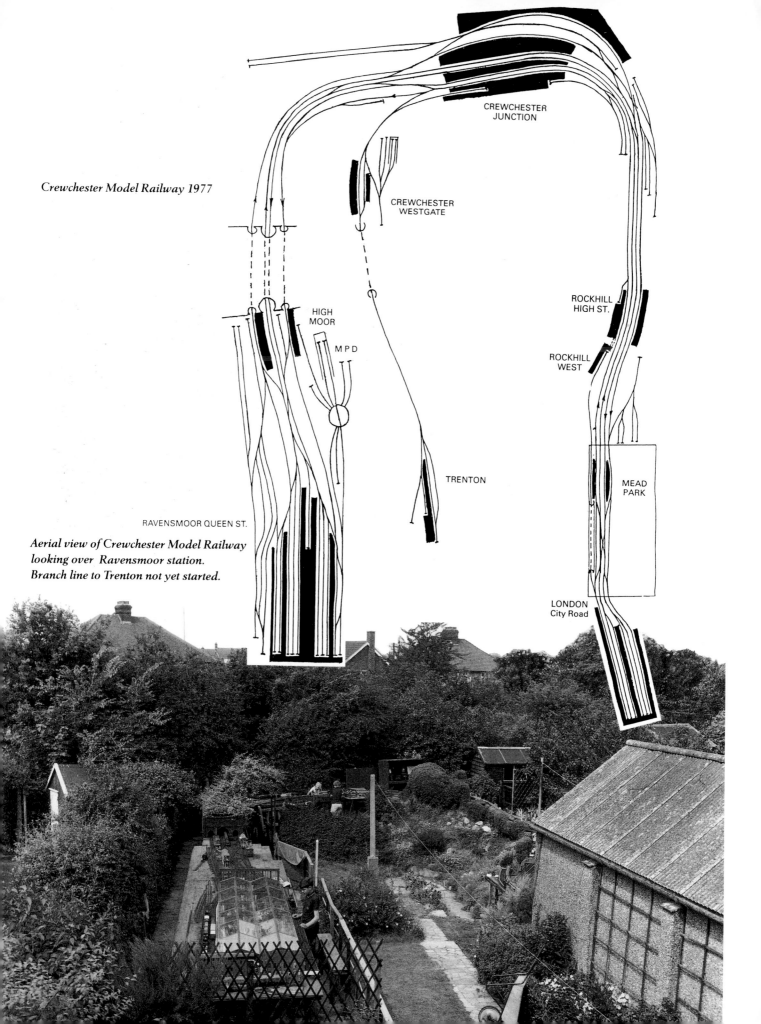

Crewchester Model Railway 1977

CREWCHESTER
JUNCTION

CREWCHESTER
WESTGATE

HIGH
MOOR

MPD

ROCKHILL
HIGH ST.

ROCKHILL
WEST

TRENTON

MEAD
PARK

RAVENSMOOR QUEEN ST.

*Aerial view of Crewchester Model Railway
looking over Ravensmoor station.
Branch line to Trenton not yet started.*

LONDON
City Road

The exhibition model railway in Model Land, New Romney, on the RH&D Railway. In the foreground, train of LNER teak stock from the Crewchester Model Railway.

Photo J.L. Ray

Although I had visited the Romney, Hythe and Dymchurch Railway in Kent on a number of occasions, it was not until the late 1960s that I was able to get to know it and the people who ran it really well. My working base when I began to haunt the RH&DR was an hotel in Ashford, but during the summer months I sought an alternative in New Romney, which would give me more time in the evenings. George Barlow, who had been with the railway since the early days of Captain Howey, and was now locomotive supremo, thought he could help, and led me from the loco shed where we had been chatting, to a very large bungalow lying close by, entering through what was obviously the back garden gate. It turned out to be a private hotel, and George introduced me to the proprietress as an old friend, resulting in my being given the best room in the establishment. The place had once been Captain Howey's house, and, George told me, the room I occupied was once Mrs Howey's bedroom. It was rather pleasant to wake up in the mornings to the sound of engines being prepared for the road.

Also at New Romney was a public exhibition Gauge 0 model railway, originally designed by Henry Greenly, and still running, operated by Jack Scrivener. Jack and I soon became good friends, and many an afternoon, as soon as the schools were closed and I was free, I would hurry there to take over the controls while Jack was able to get on with some urgent maintenance and repair work

in his workshop. Jack was a jovial character, full of fun, and when I took a party of Crewchester members down there one weekend, every one of them took a turn on the controls up on the lofty dais overlooking the entire complex. Sometimes I would take a case of Crewchester coaches with me to run on that line, once with a rather amusing result.

One evening I was in charge of the railway when a party of schoolgirls entered, obviously from one of the many rather expensive private schools in the area. Dressed in smart uniforms of brown and gold, complete with straw boaters, these young ladies were in the charge of a teacher, and having recently seen the film of St Trinians I prepared myself for the worst. I need not have worried however for the girls' behaviour was exemplary. In due course my own set of LNER teak coaches came into view and drew up into the main station. I took the opportunity to leave the dais and walk round there to re-rail a wagon which had buffer-locked on a siding. As I lifted out the glass panel to reach it, one of the girls asked the teacher "Where is Ravensmoor, Miss?" Well, they do not make them private school teachers for nothing, for without a moment's hesitation – "Oh, I think you will find Ravensmoor not far from Carlisle, dear." I must admit I was rather pleased by that, for the name was chosen to suit a purely imaginary town somewhere between Newcastle and Carlisle!

J.L.R. at the console of the Gauge 0 railway in Model Land, New Romsey. 1970.

During the few years I was able to pay periodic visits to that part of the country, my visits to the railway were touched with both comedy and tragedy. Jack Scrivener was always good fun and we enjoyed many a laugh, often over the comments heard from visitors, and in the evenings, when the model railway was closed I would wander over to the engine sheds and watch George Barlow put his beloved locomotive *Green Goddess* to bed before repairing to the inn nearby, now re-named 'The Captain Howey', where we would lower the odd pint or two and exchange yarns. I had heard from several sources that footplate passes were virtually non-existent on the RH&DR for there was little room on the footplate of those Greenly engines, and a very intensive service had to be kept running. I was all the more surprised therefore when George offered me a footplate trip over the entire railway one evening, and I was given an official footplate pass. On that evening George was driving one of the American outline locomotives, *Dr Syn*, and it was on this that I rode from New Romney to Hythe, turned the engine on the turntable and then ran back to Dungeness and finally to New Romney.

Another man I got to know very well there was Peter Hobson, a man who had retired from the Army and set his hand to any task on the railway; driving, signalling, shed-work – anything to do with his beloved steam engines. He lived in a beautiful old Elizabethan house in New Romney, and on several occasions we went there to operate his extensive Gauge 0 railway in the huge loft of the house. There we would sit and watch the trains as we quaffed quantities of Peter's ale. Much of his coaching stock came from the same source as mine, namely Fred Newman, and indeed he had one LMS set precisely similar to my own main line set. One evening as I was about to depart, Peter brought out a box of bits and pieces. "I have been saving these for Crewchester" he explained "– if they are any use to you. I don't want them." In that box were three Bing six-coupled mechanisms and two early Bassett-Lowke four-coupled – all in perfect working order. Peter must have known that these were highly marketable and would fetch high prices, especially the Bing, which were quite the best clockwork mechanisms ever produced, but he refused to take any money. It had to content myself with slipping a large treasury note into his daughter's money box before I left. It was a most timely and valuable contribution to Crewchester stores, and typical of this generous man. I drove home bearing the precious mechanisms,

showing them to the members of the Crewchester Club the next morning where it was decided to send an official letter of thanks to Peter. On Sunday morning I was woken by my wife who had a newspaper in her hand. "Someone on the Romney, Hythe, and Dymchurch Railway has died" she told me. I assumed that it was a man whom I had met and who had already suffered several heart-attacks, but when I read the paper in more detail I saw to my horror that it was Peter.

The following morning I hastened back to New Romney to find the entire staff in a state of shock and distress, for Peter had been a popular man. Mr Snell, the overall manager of the line told me that he had been on his way home on Friday evening when he heard the news on his car radio and turned back immediately to find what had happened. Apparently, Peter was on driving duty that day and was taking *Samson* (which he always referred to as 'Sammy') back on the last train to Hythe. There was a fine drizzle falling at the time and as the train approached the unmanned level crossing not far from Dymchurch station, a car driven by youths who were being chased by the police, struck the engine as it passed over the level crossing. It swayed as Peter tried to stand up, but he was impeded by the weather-sheet slung from cab roof to tender, his leg was pinned as the tender telescoped on to the engine, and then the engine fell on to its side with Peter pinned helplessly. To make matters worse, a steam valve burst, directing a jet of scalding steam on to Peter's chest. It took some time for an ambulance to arrive, and he died on the way to hospital. I believe the youths responsible got off with a light sentence! Later, I was told by Ann, Peter's wife, that she had no photograph of her husband, a gap that I was fortunately able to fill. I also have cine film showing Peter working at New Romney shed.

Before leaving the 1960s, a further digression might not be out of place, for yet again that strange series of coincidences connected with the late Rev Parley of Norfolk continued. Tom Dack had on a number of occasions asked me if I knew what happened to "that big blue engine" of Parley's, but with that rather vague description even Arthur Dewar could throw no light upon the mystery. When I was giving a talk in Norwich, one of the audience told me that he had once been to Parley's railway at Tivetshall, and had been most interested to see slides of the engines which had once worked there. "But" he asked "do you know what happened to the big blue engine which used to run on that line?" Even this gentlemen could give no more detailed description. And then I had a letter from another parson, named Turnbull, living in Suffolk. He had once been to visit Crewchester many years before, and now, he told me, he was getting too old and frail to run his huge Gauge 0 railway in an outhouse in his back garden; would I care to come and see it before it was dismantled?

Taking one of the Crewchester members with me, I drove to the Suffolk village and found the address where Rev Turnbull greeted me and took me to this large building where his railway was. He was indeed a very old man then, extremely shaky and a trifle absent-minded, but although much of the track had rusted beyond redemption and no maintenance had been carried out for a considerable time, he did manage to get some trains moving. There were many items of ancient tinplate construction which were rusting away, and I did suggest that he ought to get something done about preserving or even selling them before they were beyond repair. Just before we left, he told me there was one engine I had not yet seen, and he would open the shed and get in out. From the shed came a huge over-scale model of *Cardean*, in Caledonian blue livery, with the paint badly crazed and peeling off. The engine was powered by a Walker Fenn mechanism which was quite unserviceable, but it was quite an impressive model. When I asked him where he obtained this model he replied "Oh, that came from an old friend of mine, long since dead; chap named Parley." So that was the missing "big blue engine"!

When I asked him if he wished to sell it he replied that he wanted to sell everything, but he seemed unwilling to discuss a price. "The thing won't run" he said "So you'd better have it – it's no good to me." When we went into the house, his wife, Lady Jane, told me that her husband was getting very confused about things and that it was no use trying to talk business with him, so I showed her the engine and told her that it might be worth quite a fair amount if it could be repaired and repainted. She said "You give him five pounds for it and he will be delighted; he did so enjoy Crewchester when he came to see you."

When I got the engine home and removed the huge Walker Fenn mechanism I found that one of the springs carrying the counterweights (bobs) was broken, leaving two unbalanced springs still intact. John Hart made up a new leaf for me and I got the engine to run, but the trouble was that with the great steam-roller wheels and over-scale size of the body, the engine could never run on my line. However, I stripped all the crazed (almost black) paint off, and repainted the engine as best I could so that it looked a little less disreputable, and I would sometimes run it along a length of track where there were no points and no platforms, just for the pleasure of watching it move again after all these years.

A year later I had a phone call from a lady who told me that she was the daughter of the late Rev Turnbull, and that her mother had mentioned that Jack Ray had bought *Cardean*. Her father had died recently, and could she come and have one more look at the engine she used to drive as a little girl? She did come and I did run the engine along track which had no obstacles for the oversized engine and the lady was delighted. "I used to clean the wheels of that engine when I was a child" she told me – it is so good to see it running again."

Towards the end of the decade we began to hear a persistent cry from the members of the Crewchester Club, "When are we going to have the branch?" There was no doubt that the boys really looked forward to Crewchester Junction really becoming a true junction, but Ravensmoor had to take priority, being on the main line. Fred Newman had built me an LMS push-pull coach early in the 1960s, but pending the Trenton branch it had gone to John Hart's line to work the Oakleigh branch, usually powered by either the little Bassett-Lowke 0-6-0 No. 112 or later by a Webb 'Coal' tank. No. 112 was a bit of model railway history, for the number had been taken from Bassett-Lowke's London address: 112, High Holborn.

Push-pull train at the timber-built 'down' platform, Crewchester (Westgate) station on the Vale of Trenton line.

The new turntable at Ravensmoor.
Black Five passes with a 'down' express bound for Ravensmoor.

There was still much work to be done at Ravensmoor, with engine sheds to be built, a turntable to be installed (a major headache on an outdoor railway) and goods yards to be laid out, so it was not until 1970 that any real progress was made on the Valve of Trenton branch. A start was made however by building the other Crewchester station, Crewchester Westgate. I have always rather enjoyed the idea of two stations for the same town; it is a lovely bit of extravagance! Yet it follows prototype practice and many examples could be cited. Westgate was to be a modest sized station, with two goods roads and a two-road engine shed, and with a passing loop on the branch line. The story we cooked up for it was that originally Westgate had only one platform, obviously signalled for two-way running on the single track branch, but when Trenton became a popular marina, and also the Trenton Chemical Works opened there in the 1930s, the little station proved to be something of a bottle-neck, so, grudgingly, the LMS provided a timber-built platform on a passing loop.

Mention had been made of a turntable at Ravensmoor, suggesting that such a feature is a problem. Turntables are very extravagant of space and are not the easiest of things to get working well. For a long time I hovered between a turntable and a triangle until John Hart offered to build the essential components for me, using a worm and gear operated by a crank handle protruding from the side of the baseboard. The platform of the table was built of solid brass, and today that turntable is still working well; but then everything John did worked well! Engines had to move over the turntable to reach the shed – rarely correct practice, but forced upon us – and it completed a quite sizeable MPD for the terminus.

After this shed had been in service for several years I built an extension to the baseboard and added three more engine roads, carrying out this work during the week. When the boys arrived on Saturday I asked them to go and have a look round Ravensmoor to see if they could spot any change. Out of eight boys, all familiar with the layout, only one spotted the new loco roads! This I took as something of a compliment for the new roads did actually look as if they had been there for years.

And so the 1960s drew to a close, with Ravensmoor now fully operational, and the promise of that long-awaited branch line from Crewchester likely to be redeemed very shortly. Membership was still holding up and attendances satisfactory, so there was no real sign yet of the great changes which were to affect the railway so drastically.

Above:
Headed by Fowler 4F, a pickup goods leaves Crewchester and faces the climb to Greystone summit. This engine, now electrified, was the last locomotive to be commissioned in clockwork days and was built by Bob Lovell. One can imagine how, seconds after this picture was taken, the driver would open his regulator for the hard work ahead, and a column of smoke would billow upwards from the chimney.

Below:
A distinguished visitor to Crewchester. THE PORTS EXPRESS was built specifically by Eddie Bye to run between his own STONEMOUTH DOCKS and PORT TRENTON on my line. As we live 120 miles apart this does cause a few raised eyebrows – but here is the train, headed by T9 arriving in Crewchester Junction, where it will reverse and travel down the branch to Port Trenton behind a Crewchester engine, while the T9 is serviced as the guest of Crewchester MPD.

The old clockwork CAMERONIAN and
compounds have long since gone from
Crewchester. They have been replaced
however by two scratch-built models in 12v
2-rail. Midland compound 1032 pilots
Fowler Royal Scot 4-6-0 No. 6113
CAMERONIAN on a north-bound
express. A group of admirers stands on
platform 1, while the driver of 1032 has a
final oil-round before departure.

Right:
Aerial view of today's RAVENSMOOR
showing that road-bridge spanning the
throat of the station. (For full lurid story –
see text!) The tracks on the left are in fact
the approaches to Rockhill, visually
separated by the high barrier running right
down the garden.

DAVID L. SMITH

The 1970s were the last decade of my working life. They were also the last years of the Crewchester Model Railway Club as it had existed for over a quarter of a century. But they were good years, with further development on the railway, new friends made, and a time when one could still look forward with reasonable certainty to a future. Before turning once again to the story of Crewchester, however, let me indulge in yet another of my digressions. It concerns one of the most remarkable men I have ever met and with whom I developed a firm friendship, and to tell this story I must back-track a little into the 1960s and even further.

In the days when I stayed in Surbiton with John Hart I found on my bedside table a number of books, not surprisingly on railway topics. Pride of place was given to a volume entitled *Tales of the Glasgow and South Western Railway* by David L Smith. The stories had originally been published during the early 1940s in the *Railway Magazine*, where I had read some of them, and I had been fascinated by the writer's highly individual style as well as his subject matter. A copy of the same book lay in the bedroom I occupied when I stayed with Arthur Dewar in Lincolnshire. I found that John Hart shared my admiration and affection for this volume, and we would frequently sit up into the small hours, discussing the tales and speculating upon the author, for something of a mystery surrounded him.

John and I would read aloud certain favourite extracts, relishing the way in which the author brought his characters to life, but we could not determine exactly what manner of man David L Smith was – or even if he still lived. He wrote with the precision of an historian and the style of a poet at times so as to suggest that he was a man of letters rather than of the footplate. Yet no clue was forthcoming as to just what role he played on the railway which he so obviously loved. A letter to him care of his publishers brought no reply and we learned later that it never reached him, so we assumed that he was dead. After all, he wrote authoritatively about events towards the end of the last century, so it was not unreasonable to assume that he remembered them.

One day, I received a cutting from a Glasgow newspaper, sent to me by one of my colleagues at Collins, reporting a talk given to a packed audience in the Paisley Railway Institute by David L Smith – so he was alive, and obviously active. Then occurred one of those coincidences to which I have often alluded. Ross Mackie, one of John's 'railway boys', now grown up, was travelling in Scotland and traced David L Smith to an address near Ayr. Knowing of my interest, and being a keen reader of 'The Tales' himself, Ross gave me the address and I was able to contact the elusive writer. The outcome was that I received a cordial invitation to call upon David Smith when next I was in Glasgow, which was in 1970. Arriving at his bungalow about three miles out of Ayr on the Maybole Road, I was greeted by a frail-looking gentleman whose slight frame was oddly ill-matched to the vibrant and resonant voice: "You are welcome – come away in and meet my wife."

His wife (Margaret) and he had been married barely three years, and David was 71 at the time I met him. Their 'Best Man' had been the well-known writer, G. Freeman Allen, who had persuaded David to collect the articles from the *Railway Magazine* and publish them in book form. An entire book could be written about that first evening, for I persuaded David to tell me about himself and how he came to write 'The Tales'. Knowing how closely I would be catechised by other readers of his book when I returned south, I hung upon every word. Summarised, I learned that David had been born in Dalmellington, a village at the head of the Doon Valley (Burns: 'Ye Banks and Braes o' bonnie Doon') in 1899, the son of the Headmaster of Dalmellington Upper School, who held a Master of Arts degree, and this explained why David had such facility with words. David had suffered from a debilitating malaise which kept him often from school and prevented his taking up either a University course, or indeed any form of career. About this he was very sensitive and preferred not to dwell upon that period, yet it is necessary to mention it for it explains why he had so much time to haunt his local railway station, the little terminus at Dalmellington.

Fortunately, his illness did not often keep him abed, but he could undertake no strenuous work. Very quickly be became a familiar figure to the railwaymen, who adopted him almost as one of themselves and gradually he began to take footplate trips, going further and further until his journeys covered almost the entire G&SWR system. Although he sought official sanction from the authorities, this was never forthcoming, and if, on his trips, officialdom reared its head, he would have to "coorie doon" or make himself scarce. David's family were well known in the Doon Valley, for his forebears had been influential in the mining industry (both of iron and coal), so with his father, Headmaster of the local school, most of the railwaymen would know him.

A natural raconteur, David held me enthralled as each question of mine brought forth yet another 'Tale' of the G&SWR; yet throughout the evening there was an air of almost puzzlement that his life was of such interest to men in the south that one should travel far to hear of it. He was one of the most genuinely modest men I knew, yet totally without the affected self-deprecation which disguises self-esteem, and this was illustrated during the meal Margaret had prepared for us. I had been speaking of John Hart, both as a model railway man, a driver on the Bluebell Railway in Sussex, and the man himself. When I told him of how John and I were so familiar with David's stories that we could almost recite certain sections by heart, and then proceeded to do so, quoting a whole paragraph, he fell silent, his knife and fork lying idle on his plate. The section I recited was one of John's and my favourites, and it told of Saturday 16th November 1918 (David invariably quoted dates, places and names – he was never vague about facts).

"We were in high heart that night, for the war was over and we thought that a great peace had come to the world. It will come yet, and maybe on that glad night the ghost of little 231 will return to the Doon Valley and go soaring up in the moonlight with her exhaust echoing from the silent hills, her high column of sparks leaping to the stars, and the gallant little heart of her singing with a great joy."

Davie looked at me. "Your words" he murmured in that soft south-western Scottish lilt, "are like water to a thirsty man. I had no idea my writings were known so far away."

The evening passed all too quickly, and so, unsure of whether these people went early or late to bed, at about ten o'clock I began to take my leave. John Hart had been a main topic of conversation, especially when Davie realised that he was still driving steam engines on the Bluebell Railway in Sussex, but John did not know of my arrangements to meet David; so, seeing a phone in the hall, I asked David if I might use it. Dialling John's Surbiton number, his voice came over as clearly as if it were a local call, and the following conversation took place.

"Hullo, John. Can you guess where I am?"

"Oh – let me see – September – oh, probably on some wild Scottish moor I would think."

"I am in the home of David Smith. I have just spent the evening with him."

"You never have! You lucky so-and-so – you must tell me all about it when you come over next."

"John, David is here beside me and wants a word with you" – and with that I handed the instrument to David.

Later, John told me that the sound of that musically resonant voice over the phone, speaking to him as to an old friend, was extremely moving – for to him David was indeed an old friend, known through his books. There were other books by David which we both possessed, some of them technical, others historical; but none quite matched 'The Tales' in our affections.

There followed a number of visits to Davie and his wife, whenever I was in Scotland, sometimes just spending the evening with them, and others when we would venture out, as on the glorious summer day when we drove along the whole route of the line from Ayr to Stranraer, calling at every station en route, each one of which was a familiar name to me. Girvan, Barrhill, and over the bleak Chirmorie, past 'the Gunner's' and 'the Swan's Neck' cuttings, down to New Luce, where we had tea in a quaint little shop in the tiny village; Pinwherry, and so on, then back along the Galloway coast with Ailsa Craig wearing a lace-cap of cloud in the misty sea. On one of these visits Davie (as he was known to his friends) allowed me to put a small portable cassette-recorder on the table in front of the settee where we sat and thus I now have some three hours of unpublished tales of the G&SWR.

When he and Margaret spent a holiday in London, we arranged a meeting with John Hart, and the four of us drove out to the hotel where I was staying in St Albans where we dined together – the only occasion when we were all four together. It was a memorable evening. David is no longer with us, but for fifteen years I enjoyed his friendship and have kept all his beautifully written letters, full of anecdote, as well as that precious tape, and as a small tribute to a remarkable man I have made a Gauge 0 Guild slide/cassette programme on the life and times of David L Smith.

In Scotland his name is still venerated, but that fame is not confined to Scotland, for when I was spending one of those evenings in New Romney with George Barlow, he mentioned the name of David L Smith, telling me that he had actually once met the man. "He wouldn't remember me," said George "but I gave a talk to his Glasgow and South Western Society years ago. We met only briefly. He is a wonderful man. I was so glad to have met him." On my tape, made in Davie's home, I mention the remark by George, and Davie replied. "Oh aye – I remember George Barlow well. A decent man – he gave us a talk at the Institute, and very good it was too." I sent George a copy of the tape, which delighted him. All the time I knew Davie he took a great interest in Crewchester for he had, in his younger days, built a Gauge 0 model railway of his own. All the Crewchester members were conversant with 'The Tales' and quite often some incident on the line would call forth a relevant quotation from that well-loved book.

7

THE VALE OF TRENTON BRANCH AND CREWCHESTER'S SILVER JUBILEE

In the days when Britain was honeycombed with railways and it was possible to travel almost anywhere by train, the junction station was a familiar part of almost any journey. Leaving London or any other big city in the splendour of a main line express hauled by some majestic monster of an engine, the time would come when one was deposited on some station, possibly out in the heart of the country, where the express would pause briefly before going on to another important city. Possibly the connection would be waiting in a bay platform, often a picturesque assortment of ancient coaches headed by an archaic locomotive which, after service elsewhere, had been put out to grass on this branch line. There was a sense of abandonment as the passenger tried to adapt from the comfortable convenience of the main line corridor train with its restaurant car, to the rather more austere conditions of the branch line train; a sense of adventure too, as if leaving some known way for an unknown hinterland along unfrequented byways. In the case of a traveller going in the opposite direction, the converse was true.

It was this sort of atmosphere I wanted to create at Crewchester Junction, an important north midland town where most trains – even the expresses – usually stopped. Over on the down side, alongside platform 6 was a bay at the north end of that platform, bounded by the wall of the high-level road from the station

entrance. From the bay a single line swung away westwards, disappearing under the road bridge and emerging at Crewchester Westgate station. Beyond Westgate the single line entered West-gate tunnel, after which it ran down the Vale of Trenton before ending at the small terminus of Trenton. But it was not until well into 1970 that this branch was completed and our push-pull train came into its rightful role, plying between Junction and Trenton. It was also about this time that John Blair's visits became less frequent for a number of reasons, the principal one being the acquisition of his own house in Hertfordshire and all the added responsibilities attached to house ownership. But John had played an important part in the development of Crewchester and had contributed a great deal in both material ways and in ideas. We did not always see eye to eye, but that is natural in any human relations; John preferring to work the railway with just the two of us rather than the crowd of schoolboys, while I wanted as many people as possible to share in our hobby. But the 200 mile round trip to visit Ipswich became a problem as John did not possess a car, and the rail journey was complicated and inconvenient.

Ralph Cooper was Chairman of the Barnet (Herts) Model Rail-way Club, about whose layout Ralph had written several articles in the model press. In addition to this, Ralph had in his loft an extensive 00 model railway of his own. 'Extensive' must be one of the understatements of all time!

The branch terminus, Trenton in
1974. Above, the push-pull train
awaits departure time in the bay
while the branch goods stands in
the siding.

Trenton station between trains
on a damp morning soon after
the branch was completed.

Trenton Chemical Works industrial saddletank Norah *brings in a short goods train to Trenton, having collected it from Westgate yards.*

Trenton station looking east towards Crewchester Junction.

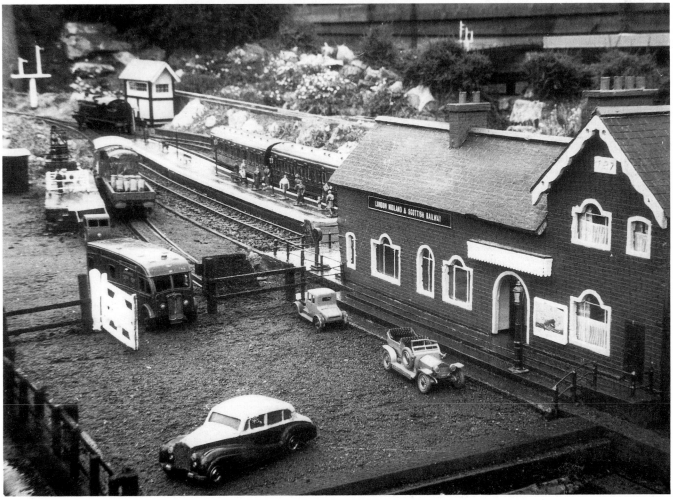

My first visit was on my own, leading to many further trips to Barnet with car-loads of Crewchester MRC members who quickly adopted the railway as their favourite visiting place. The loft was a large one and contained quite the most bewildering mass of 00 railway I have ever seen.

Starting in one corner, there was a big terminus, quite obviously copied as faithfully as space would permit from King's Cross, including 'Top Shed' and Ferme Park Goods Depot. The big signal box just outside the station was clearly recognisable, as was Gasworks tunnel, but what really caught my eye was the number of locomotives and assortment of rolling stock. Very few model railway shops would stock the sheer quantity and variety of engines and coaches which I saw on that railway. For instance, at 'Top Shed' (and the loco sidings between the platforms and Gasworks tunnel), there would be two or three A4s, a couple of A3s, a B12, two or three N2 0-6-2Ts, 'Klondyke' small-boilered Atlantic – plus the large-boilered version – and so forth; but this pattern was repeated, more or less, at every shed as far north as Doncaster. Two or three Pullman sets, the usual array of Gresley main line teak and some ECJS coaches, not to mention suburban and cross-country sets, were always present and then, in the goods depot, there was everything from coal wagons to fitted van trains. The picture was quite complete! Leaving King's Cross, the line ran through a 90° curve, along the wall to the far end of the room, through yet another 90° turn, passing over the Nene bridge to enter Peterborough North, modelled on the old station with its train shed. North of Peterborough was the familiar brick-arch bridge spanning the entire track layout and another 90° turn to run along the other side of the loft, dropping to a lower level as it passed under King's Cross station; then another turn and the line reached Grantham.

From Grantham, a branch left the main line north of the station to reach Nottingham in the middle of the room, while the main line crept under Peterborough station, along the end of the room to emerge onto the far side of the room alongside the Peterborough-Grantham stretch, where the next station was Newark. Still climbing, the line passed again under King's Cross and when it reached the long stretch of straight, came to Retford. Here again a branch swung westwards to Sheffield, built in the middle of the room. The line, now at high level ran round through another 180° before coming to what I thought was the northern terminus of Doncaster, again copied carefully from the prototype. Some fifteen to twenty more engines would be seen on shed there, but that was far from the end of the story. Hidden from view, the main line continued right round the room until it reached a point somewhere near that Nene bridge south of Peterborough station – now far below the level of the northbound line. It then entered a tunnel bored in the wall of the house, and came out next door! There dwelt Ralph's nephew, also a railway fan, and in his loft the line divided, one route going via York, and the other via Leeds and Harrogate, finally coming to the extreme northern terminus of Newcastle. One day we timed a non-stop train from Newcastle to London; it took eight minutes!

The immediate question which sprang to mind, apart from the frightening maintenance work-load, was how this vast system was operated, to which Ralph replied that members of the Barnet MRC came round, but that the sessions too often turned into competitions between the various operators to see who could cause the most chaos by bunging trains to the next section as fast as possible. He was working on a timetable, but on such a vast system this was not easy – meanwhile the rather haphazard working continued. Very soon I organised a visit from the Crewchester

members and they took to the railway like a duck to water. As they were all conversant with block bell codes, they simply adapted these to verbal exchanges, thus one would hear King's Cross calling out to Peterborough: "Peterborough, four?" and Peterborough would respond with "Four, London." A few moments later King's Cross would call: "Peterborough, two", to which would come the reply "Two, London." The train would then leave King's Cross and run along to Peterborough. Ralph looked on in amazement, not understanding what was going on, but drinking it all in. When we retired for refreshment he told me "I have never in my life seen a model railway run like that. You must come and instruct my chaps."

For many years we made pilgrimages to Barnet to work that marvellous layout which now has had to be dismantled owing to a move of house. The principle Ralph worked on was basically simple in the extreme although the tracks were complicated. Owing to the pitch of the roof it was impossible to provide scenery along the main line, but when a station was approached there would be a full signalling with lineside effects and buildings to add realism to the scene. All points were mechanically operated from either lever frames by the track or by single trackside levers at ground level. Up, Down, and sidings were all colour-coded so that it was easy to identify point-controls. One or two inaccessible points a long way from the operator's position would be electrically worked, but these were the exception. All red levers were Up and blue were Down; yellow were sidings, with crossovers between up and down being two-coloured. It took very little time to learn any of the operating positions and all our visits were memorable as some of the most enjoyable events of the year.

At one time Ralph had modelled in Gauge 0 and he had a considerable amount of rolling stock and locomotives which had lain idle for many years. One of these was a magnificent large boilered Ivatt Atlantic, built from scratch in $^1/_{16}$in brass, and weighing 5lbs. The builder, more accustomed to making live-steam passenger-carrying engines, had not been too successful in making this clockwork-powered engine run, and Ralph gave it to me on 'permanent loan' to see what could be done with it. It was beyond me, for the problem lay in those close-set driving wheels. The main difficulty lay in the fact that to place the keyhole in the right place, the key would have to pass right through the coils of the spring! And so the engine went to Bob Lovell, the miracle-worker. After a while the engine returned, repainted in LNER green, and powered by a Bassett-Lowke four-coupled clockwork mechanism. Bob had turned the mechanism round the 'wrong way' so that it protruded into the cab, with its leading end now between the rear driving wheels and its rear end lying between the trailing wheels under the cab, giving very tight clearances and allowing virtually no side-play in the trailing wheels. The engine had taken on some semblance of a 4-6-0 in that the two pairs of drivers and the trailing wheels were an almost rigid chassis. But the engine ran well right up to the end of clockwork days, being returned to Ralph (very reluctantly) when we went two-rail.

Among all that long-stored collection we discovered the body of a GNR 4-4-2T, in LNER days known as Class C12. It was in a bad state, with the condensing apparatus missing, although the holes in the side-tanks and boiler were there, and this Ralph said he was going to throw out. Some years later he gave it to me and it lay for quite a while on a shelf under my railway. One day I took it out, scraped the mess of horrible green paint off and found underneath all that 'gunge' a very nicely made model. I had a new chassis and wheels built for her and painted the engine in GNR livery, for no special reason except that I liked it that way.

The steel overall roof at Ravensmoor and my son, Stuart.   E.A.D.T.

There was still that little matter of the overall roof at Ravensmoor. Grateful as we were to Frank Vaux for making the rafters for the 'bedstead' roof, I wanted something more closely resembling Barlow's magnificent single-span roof at St Pancras, and my enquiries led me to another of these people who seem to appear, as John Hart had said "out of the pavement in front of me". There was a local blacksmith, apparently, who was now semi-retired and who would undertake odd jobs for organisations such as Scouts, Guides, and other youth groups, provided they would give him time, such jobs being relegated to his 'spare time'. It was a difficult job to find the address which lay up a cart-track known as 'The Drift', but eventually I found Mr Whiting, a slow-spoken, even slower-moving man of well past middle-age, who greeted me cautiously and then asked what he could do for me – I told him.

For some ten minutes Mr Whiting ruminated on what I had said – that I wanted a steel framework for an overall roof for my terminus, and then he ventured, "You do me some plans and we'll see. Good afternoon." Wondering just what I had let myself in for, I went back home, did a set of drawings with full specification and took them back to Mr Whiting. He regarded them for a long time,

and then said "You leave these with me and I'll see what I can do with them." Not long afterwards there came a message that my roof was ready for collection. So, making my way back to 'The Drift', I once again presented myself to Mr Whiting, who led me to a large outhouse in the corner of which stood an odd assortment of steel strips, rods, nuts, bolts and metal strapping. By now I had learned that it was best not to hurry Mr Whiting, so I left him to open the batting. He looked at the pile of components for a while as if trying to remember just what they were, and then spoke: "I've made them like you said, and that should be all right. It all screws together like a giant Meccano set, and I have added some reinforcement strapping for the bow-string girders – that's made them good and firm. You've got half-inch steel rods for uprights, tapped at one end, so you stick them through your baseboard with a nut either side and nothing will shift that roof." This conscientious man had even painted all the parts with a red primer, and now I waited to learn the cost.

Workmanship of that order does not come cheap, and goodwill like this is rare. Treading as delicately as I could, and trying not to rush him, I asked him what I owed him. He stood looking at me for

57

almost two minutes, as if weighing up what I could afford, and I rather regretted the lounge suit, wishing I had adopted worn jeans and a frayed shirt collar. At last he said "Well now, if I charge you twenty pounds I shan't get rich and you won't get poor." It was absurdly low, but that was his price and he brooked no argument.

Later on when I had got the roof home and when it had been completed I took a photograph during a full running session and sent it to Mr Whiting with our thanks. He seemed very pleased with it.

The 1970s saw one further major development on the line – the portable extension beyond the garage which formed not only an extension of the length of run, but six additional roads which offered storage room to balance the big northern terminus. This extension had to be dismantled at night so that the garage could be locked, but in fact it took five strong men to carry it into the garage after a session. It was in effect a huge fiddle-yard, but did have four platform faces, thus acting as the London terminus of City Road. All the track inside the garage was taken up and a new system of points installed so that trains could reach any of the six roads on the extension from any of the four roads passing through the garage. In addition, a single track branch line took the place of what had been a siding against the wall, emerging from the garage where the old carriage sidings had been, and terminating in a small country single-platform station called Rockhill West.

This station was worked by the 'one-engine-in-steam' principle, and the story we fabricated to justify the line was that a branch line had been built by the Great Northern Railway from London, out through the western suburbs as far as Rockhill. Although the GNR had obtained running powers into City Road (rather as it had once been allowed to work into St Pancras), when permission was sought from the LNWR to run the branch into Rockhill High Street the GNR was met with blank refusal, and not without good reason, for it would have asking for trouble to have branch-line trains encroaching upon the 'race track' section of the main line.

The Great Northern was obliged to erect this tiny station a hundred yards up Rockhill High Street, which became known as Rockhill West. The two stations were connected by a passage way running from the down platform at Rockhill High Street to the West station.

Before leaving these clockwork days, one other man is worthy of mention in these pages, for he was an inspiration to everyone who came into contact with him. His name was Donald Wilson, who, during the 1960s used to bring parties of boys from the secondary school where he was Head of Science, to see Crewchester. One day, early in the 1970s, Don rang me to ask if he could come and renew his acquaintance with Crewchester, adding almost as an afterthought that he had lost his sight since he was last with us. His wife, Angela, drove him to Ipswich and it was a most moving sight to see him look at the railway with his fingers, for he always spoke of 'seeing' things. His railway knowledge was prodigious, especially of LNWR matters in which he specialised, and a whole chapter could be devoted to this courageous man. Just one example will illustrate what manner of man he was.

I had marshalled a number of engines on the loco road at Ravensmoor close to the edge of the baseboard where he could handle and touch them. One by one he identified them, until he came to one of my A3 Gresley Pacifics. I had left him for the moment while I sent a train off, and then he called out "What's happened to the snifting valve on this A3, Jack?" Not one of us sighted people had spotted it, but that tiny button was missing from the top of the boiler just behind the chimney. Within a week or so Don was taking over control at Ravensmoor, sitting by the block instruments, knowing what they were reading just by the sound of the needles flicking over. Nothing seemed to escape him, and soon we began to forget that he was blind. We would be asked "Have you moved that empty shock from platform 5? Well, you've got time now, so the B12 which brought the train in can be released to sheds." I once saw one of my operators, a young boy of

16 or so, openly weeping as he watched Don, laughing and enjoying every moment, working those block instruments, answering the phone, and fully in charge. If he was not working Ravensmoor he would be found at City Road where one lever frame controlled all points.

Don was a diabetic who had to spend twelve hours twice weekly on his dialysis machine, yet despite all these terrible afflictions he insisted on enjoying life. Having become accustomed to Gauge 0 at Crewchester he sold all his 00 trains and built himself an outdoor garden Gauge 0 layout, with some help from one or two of his pupils. His enthusiasm was infectious; it was impossible to be miserable when one was with him and when I introduced him to John Hart, the two men immediately became firm friends with Don spending weekends at John's house and joining in operating sessions. He would then come to Crewchester and give me a full description of almost every engine and every feature on John's line. Similarly, he went to Arthur Dewar's house and the same thing happened there.

In this context, it would be unforgivable not to mention the devotion of his wife, Angie, who not only drove him everywhere, but undertook the necessary training at Addenbrook's Hospital in order that Don could have a machine in his own home where she could tend him. Even more, she learned how to line out coaches and do many jobs beyond Don's capabilities, so that he may indulge his hobby to the full. She herself was Head of History at the same school where Don taught. More than once I heard people say "That man makes me feel ashamed of ever complaining about life's little difficulties." So it was with all of us who were privileged to know Don. When we cursed that soldering iron which would not deliver a smooth flow, we would remember Don with *his* soldering iron – and just what that entailed in terms of frustration. When he died in 1978 the Gauge 0 Guild initiated fund which rapidly reached £700, enabling two talking books for the blind to be made and dedicated to Don's memory. We have one small but very important item on the railway to remind us of Don. One of his pupils modified one of the Slater's 'huminiture' human figures to resemble Don, and then added a model of Don's guide-dog, Elsa, complete with harness. When Don died, Angie gave us that pair of figures, knowing how it had always caused amusement to Don, and we have mounted them on a plinth which now stands at Trenton Town station.

The apple green A4 Golden Eagle *ready for departure with the Pullman.*

Don Wilson

Other things happened during the 1970s which stand out in memory – not least that of George Hinchcliffe going to the USA with No. 4472 *Flying Scotsman* on its (financially) ill-fated tour. The phone call while I was staying with Arthur Dewar in Lincolnshire said everything:- George speaking from San Francisco: "I've just put 4472 on the boat for England; Bill McAlpine has baled her out." This was indeed heartening news, for the engine had been impounded pending the discharge of many huge bills for such items as coal, etc.

In 1977, the Gauge 0 Guild held its annual Convention, celebrating its twenty-first year of existence, the venue being the very fine St John's Hotel in Solihull. The day came to a close with a celebratory dinner; but for me the day was most memorable for the fact that Don Wilson came with me. No-one at that exhibition could have enjoyed themselves more than did Don, blind as he was. At every stand I would introduce him to the exhibitor, who would immediately hand their wares to Don to 'see' through his fingers. I shall never forget Freddie Cooke, the uncrowned king of live steam, handing Don model after model, and eagerly discussing the technical details as one expert to another. It was wonderful to watch people who saw Don handling the models, and see his pleasure and enjoyment reflected in their faces, as they watched him with wonder.

All the way back to Ipswich, Don was chattering excitedly like a schoolboy. Angela, his wife, told me a day or so later: "When Don came in at 2am he was radiant – I cannot remember ever seeing him so excited since his blindness. He talked for two hours, until I had to beg him to save some for the morning!"

In 1977 I suggested to the boys that as it was the silver jubilee of Crewchester, it might be fun to organise some sort of get-together of all members past and present – possibly a meal in a local pub. No sooner was the news out than we received applications for over a hundred tickets and we ended up using the Mayor's parlour in the Town Hall, Ipswich, on 12th December 1977. It turned out to be one of the happiest evenings I can ever remember, with people travelling from all over the country to be with us. 'The Visitors' toast was proposed by a founder member of the club, John Wade,

Guests of honour at the Silver Jubilee dinner of the Crewchester Model Railway Club 1977. Left to right are 'Steve' Stratten and his wife, Jack Ray and his wife, Ralph Cooper and his wife and John Hart.

E.A.D.T.

and replied to by Ralph Cooper. 'The Hobby' was proposed by my old friend Steve Stevens-Stratten, Editor of the *Model Railway Constructor*, and John Hart replied. We had no celebrities; everyone there was present because we wanted them there, and there was an atmosphere which could never be manufactured – it just happened. Even the catering manager came to me afterwards and told me that his staff had enjoyed the evening.

But things were changing at Crewchester. Attendances were falling off and recruitment was almost nil, so that at weekends it was hard to raise a quorum to operate the line. Another problem was that of getting clockwork mechanisms repaired, and in 1979 I arranged the last batch of springs for the Guild – over £3500 worth. My firm, suddenly hit by the depression, sought the support of the banks, who gave it readily, with the proviso that every employee and Director of over 60 must take early retirement – and this included me. One moment Collins were a thriving, prosperous publishing house, and overnight they were millions in the red. But those of us who had to leave were treated with incredible consideration, tempering the wind to the shorn lamb, and 1980 saw the end of my working life – and the end of twenty years of that four-track clockwork layout.

From 1980 to October 1981 I struggled on, performing feats of maintenance which left me shattered, and then one day I went down to Crewchester Junction and did a bit of stock-taking. The monster I had created was threatening to devour me and I fell into a mood of near-despair. The obvious thing to do was to sell up and invest the proceeds so as to yield some augmentation to my modest pension, and that was what I decided. I would print lists of items for sale – after all Gauge 0 was fetching high prices – and do some systematic advertising. As the cheques began to pour through my letter box I suddenly panicked. What in the name of sanity was I doing? Retirement, be it short or long, without a model railway was unthinkable. Why not use the proceeds from the sale of almost a lifetime's collection to finance a new, more modest (and manageable) railway? And this is exactly what did happen. I kept a dozen of my favourite clockwork locomotives and put the rest up for sale, together with 75% of my coaching stock, including all the Exley coaches. Now I was faced with the daunting problem of finding someone to electrify my clockwork engines, and even so, what form of current collection should I adopt? Then there was all that track to take up, another huge job; it had been put down to last a hundred years!

METAMORPHOSIS!

What was it John Hart had said about people springing up out of the pavement? There was I, knowing no more about electricity than it takes to change a light bulb, facing the prospect of building a 2-rail layout and really without a clue as to how to go about it. I was attending a model railway exhibition in Bury St Edmunds, chatting to a friend there about the proposed new line, when he pointed across the room to an exhibition layout called Wallsea.

"That is Barrie Walls. He has been made redundant and has, I know, been doing some work for Wally Mayhew and others; he might be able to help you." I had known of Barrie by repute for some time but had never actually met him, so making my way to where he was standing I introduced myself and put my problem. He heard me out and then said he thought he might be able to help me in two ways: first by converting the twelve locomotives I had retained from clockwork, and then by 'two-railing' all my passenger bogies. All the four-wheeled goods wagons had Jackson wheels which were already insulated. The agreement was that I was to let him have the engines, two at a time, and he would build new chassis, add brake-gear and cab-detail. Meanwhile I had to start work on clearing up the old layout and planning the new one.

It was at this time that my son, Stuart, went into action, working out in the gaden in quite cold weather, lifting the old track, salvaging rail chairs and rail-strip; there was no point in trying to rescue sleepers and battens, for they were soaked in years of creosote and ballast, but the rail-strip could be cleaned and re-used. Stuart's efforts, aided on some weekends by some of the Crewchester gang, meant that by January 1982 I was able to start work in the garage, laying the new track. By this time I had thought long and hard about the new layout, and had drawn up the following criteria.

1. The railway must be capable of control by as few as two people, or even one – when I was on my own.
2. Basically, it must be an end-to-end line.
3. It must incorporate an alternative out-and-back facility for the lone operator.
4. It must contain a continuous circuit for testing purposes.
5. Maintenance must lie within the capability of an old man – me!

Translating these criteria into practicalities, reference to the diagram of the railway to will show how the above stipulations were fulfilled.

1. Controllable by two people, or even one. When two people were available, one could easily handle Ravensmoor and Hartwich, for Hartwich controller is on a 15ft lead and can be placed by High Moor tunnel – only a few paces from Ravensmoor controller.
2. End-to-end. Ravensmoor, High Moor, Hartwich (Wilson Street), Crewchester Junction, and Rockhill (High Street).
3. Out and back. Trenton Town, Crewchester Junction, Hartwich Wilson Street, High Moor, Roman Wall Junction, Crewchester East and back into Trenton Town.
4. Continuous circuit. Crewchester Junction, Roman Wall Junction, Hartwich Wilson Street and Crewchester Junction.
5. Maintenance. I did not really believe this even when I wrote it!

Reconciling this to geographical accuracy demanded more than usual poetic licence, but the map will show how the Crewchester Railway does approach the outer bounds of credibility.

One device has been built into the wiring which does in fact permit one lone operator to enjoy a solitary session, and this involves having an alternative plug-in position for each of two of the operational sections, Hartwich and Rockhill. If I am on my own and want to run the railway, I plug Hartwich controller into its alternative socket at Crewchester Junction; similarly with the Rockhill controller. Ravensmoor and Hartwich Central are switched out, but this still leaves plenty of scope for running trains. One further device has helped to achieve this end – the ability to hand over control of the line between High Moor Tunnel and Roman Wall Junction to EITHER Ravensmoor OR Crewchester. This is very simply done by means of a double-pole switch whereby when the road is set from Roman Wall Junction into Ravensmoor, then Ravensmoor automatically has control of that section. Once the points are thrown for the link line between Roman Wall Junction and Crewchester, then automatically the current is controlled from Crewchester. The optional position for

Rockhill controller is again at Crewchester. So, having prepared a train for departure northwards from Rockhill, the lone operator can return to his seat at Crewchester and, with the Rockhill controller conveniently to hand, bring that train on when it is due without stirring from his seat.

But all this is to anticipate the story, for in 1982 it was still in the planning stage. Other vital decisions had to be made before even the first length of rail was laid, such as stud contact(?), two-rail(?), third rail, inside or outside(?) Here I spent much time listening to enthusiastic exponents of all these methods, before opting for two-rail, principally because of the more convincing appearance of the track where steam-outline engines were to run. One of the boys who had joined the Crewchester MRC as a young schoolboy but now has a degree in engineering, helped me over the principal electrical hurdle by drawing me a coloured diagram of how turnouts are wired for two-rail. One of life's supreme moments was that in which I drove the first two-rail engine over the first turnout – and it worked!

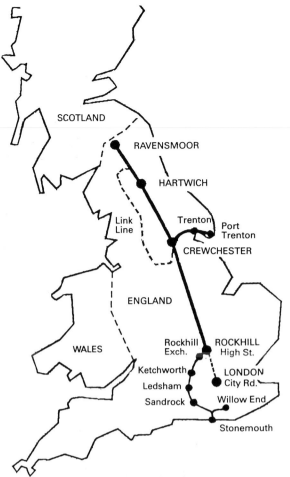

Right – The Crewchester Line showing the imaginary connection with Eddie Bye's North & South Junction Rly. on the Kent coast.

Trenton Town looking towards Port Trenton. In the distance is the lift-out viaduct linking the line in the garage to the portable extension to Port Trenton.

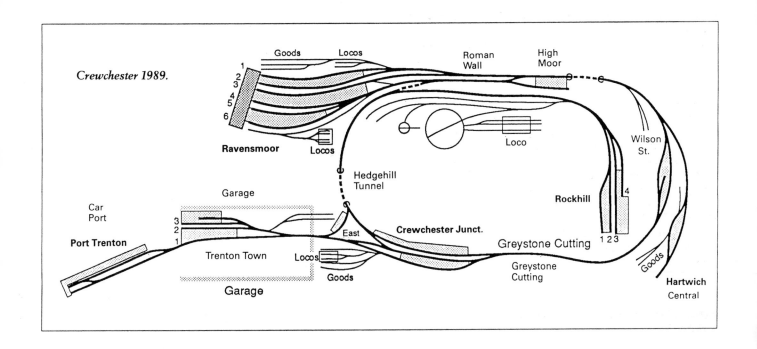

Crewchester 1989.

Goods Locos   Roman   High
                Wall   Moor

1
2
3
4
5
6

Ravensmoor   Locos

                              Wilson
                              St.

                  Hedgehill
                  Tunnel   **Rockhill**   4

Garage   1 2 3

Car   Loco
Port   3
            2   East   **Crewchester Junct.**
Port Trenton 1   **Greystone Cutting**

            Trenton Town   Locos
                                         Greystone
                            Goods   Cutting   Goods

            Garage   **Hartwich**
                                                        Central

The Class 5 leaving Ravensmoor with an LMS express.

63

Trenton Town station with the Tilbury tank in early LMS livery ready to depart for Crewchester Junction.

The quayside at Port Trenton with boat train at the platform.

Here, once again I must leave Crewchester to tell of another momentous event which occurred in 1980, the year of my official retirement from business. Early in the history of the Gauge 0 Guild, someone had had the bright idea of inviting members to submit slides of their own layouts, together with an explanatory lists, these slides all to be placed in a sort of travelling library box, available to members. This proved to be a popular service and the box travelled all over the country. In it were a few slides of Crewchester, but round about 1979 the then curator of the scheme, Roger Pound of Leicester, wrote to me pointing out that the slides of Crewchester were now fifteen years out of date, and could he have some more up-to-date material please?

With such a large model railway system I was able to provide a sequence of slides, taking viewers over the entire railway, and it was in so doing that I thought of the idea of providing a recorded commentary to accompany the slides as an alternative extra; after all, almost everyone either possesses, or has access to a cassette recorder these days. Roger was highly enthusiastic about this new approach and segregated the Crewchester set as a separate self-contained unit. Then he asked me if I could do other layouts in the same manner, so I repeated the formula on John Hart's railway and

Arthur Dewar's Highland line. The new concept immediately caught on and there was a great demand for these three sets, but Roger sent out an SOS to the effect that his work was making it impossible for him to remain as curator of the scheme, and as I was about to retire, how about me taking the whole thing over? This I did gladly, but my impending retirement was a mixed blessing in this context, for no longer would I be travelling all over Britain on business and therefore able to visit other layouts. Yet at the same time I would (in theory) have more time at my disposal.

It was at this point that another of those people popped up out of the pavement in the shape of Colin Horn, then President of the Guild. He very quickly saw that this service, if developed fully, could constitute an invaluable service to members, allowing them to 'visit' the layouts of other members without stirring from their armchairs. He quickly put the idea to the Committee and obtained official backing for the scheme, thereby relieving me of the considerable travelling expenses. Thus started the Gauge 0 Guild Slide/Cassette library in 1980 with three programmes. By 1991 it numbered 125 different programmes and today the scheme is regarded as second only in importance to the *Guild Gazette* in bringing members together and sharing interests. It was this venture which brought me into contact with many people, both well-known and unsung, giving me an insight into the world of Gauge 0 in a manner which is rare indeed. My mandate from the Committee was to lay the full cost of making new programmes at the door of the treasurer; but the lending side was to be made to pay for itself and to that end I had to undertake a costing exercise, whereby borrowers would be invited to enclose a cheque with the returned slides to cover the outward postage plus a small margin to cover overheads.

In 1981 there was another celebration – the Guild's 25th birthday – and once again a convention was laid on at the St John's Hotel in Solihull. Once again there was a dinner – at which George Hinchcliffe and I were both due to speak; but as we were at opposite ends of top table we did not have a chance to confer beforehand. Now, George Hinchcliffe is one of the most entertaining speakers I have heard, and on this occasion he was in excellent form. He started his speech with what seemed to be a survey of the current world news, touching on recent Cabinet appointments and surprises, the state of the Pound, recent developments in Russia, and so forth, and then with his audience well and truly under his spell he learned forward confidentially and in a stage-whisper asked "But have you heard the REAL news? Jack Ray is going electric!" The audience loved it, and as may be guessed, I was mercilessly ribbed about my desertion of clockwork, a cause I had passionately espoused for over thirty years.

George has the happy knack – rare in after-dinner speakers – in knowing when his audience are ahead of him and have seized the point even before his comes to it – and there he will stop. An example of this occurred in that same speech. At that time George was in charge of Steamtown at Carnforth, and he made reference to that wonderful museum as he went on – "I have been wandering round this huge exhibition today, seeing models of a standard not even dreamed of not so many years ago. Boilers perfectly aligned, cab-sides parallel and at right angles to the footplate, all verticals truly vertical – – –" then a wistful pause, and "We've nothing like that at Carnforth." He continued: "We had

The north end of Crewchester Junction station looking towards Greystone cutting and Hartwich.

Below – the south end of the station.

two Black Fives in for boiler washout, but not a lot of room to park them, so we put them side-by-side on adjacent sidings. The crane lifted the dome of the first one and could not find anywhere to put it down, so he just swung it round and dropped it on the second engine, just in front of its own dome." He paused. "He had to come along, didn't he – – – –" But already the audience was rocking with laughter as it envisaged that visitor gaping up at the Black Five with two domes – and then asking awkward questions!

By the end of 1982, less than twelve months after laying the first length of track for the new two-rail system, I was round as far as the site of Ravensmoor and the section between Trenton and Hart-wich (at the bottom of the garden where the old clockwork Crewchester Junction had been) was fully scenic, including a rocky defile called Greystone cutting where the line was supposed to pass over the Chilton Hills (sic!). The speed with which the new line progressed was in great measure due to Stuart's efforts, working ahead of me and clearing the path of a mass of accumulated mixtures of tar, creosote, ballast, encrusted dirt and roofing felt, stripping it all right down to the original baseboard which was in as good condition as the day I laid it nearly thirty years before.

Crewchester Junction was to be in quite a different place from its other sites; that city has been moved so many times over the past thirty years that the inhabitants could well be described as 'of no fixed abode'. First at Kelvedon, then half way down the left hand side of the garden at Ipswich; next, at the bottom of the garden, and now just outside the garage, occupying the site of what had been Rockhill High Street station. No useful purpose would be served by detailing the mistakes I made, necessitating at least three re-builds of the station layout; the road to Ravensmoor, like Hell, was paved with good intentions. Remembering Norris' advice to me – never build dead straight track if you can avoid it, I

caused the line to run through a series of reverse curves, all of large radius, on its way down to Hartwich, the rocky terrain giving credence to the tortuous route. At Greystone summit, where towering rocks hang above the single line, I placed a stag, usually referred to as 'The Monarch of the Glen' and there he stands to this day, presumably a keen train-spotter.

Dropping down from Greystone summit (which is in fact not a summit, for the track is level throughout; but it is a nice conceit!), the line enters wooded country, with Greystone Woods hanging on the skyline to the east, and the cutting gradually dropping down to open heathland as the line swings through a great curve over Hartwich Heath approaching Hartwich (Wilson Street) station. The name was coined to commemorate two people closely associated with Crewchester, the late John Hart, and Don Wilson, and the northern industrial town had two stations. Wilson Street lay on the outskirts of the town and comprised one long island platform with a bay at the southern end. Just north of Wilson Street station, a junction in a trailing direction leads back, past the rear of Wilson Street right into the town of Hartwich, and is known as Hartwich Central. Although possessing a short passenger platform and boasting a somewhat sporadic passenger service, mainly from Ravensmoor, Central is primarily a goods depot, with goods shed and sidings for quite a number of vans and wagons. North of Wilson Street Junction are further sidings which are now derelict, but sometimes pressed into service for the odd vehicle which cannot find room at Central. Originally there was a small engine shed there, but it was so little used that all Hartwich locomotives are now stabled at Ravensmoor. Draped over one of the buffer stops on these abandoned sidings is the wreck of a carelessly loose-shunted coal wagon, and there is lies for all time, no-one seeming to feel inclined to do anything about it.

Hartwich Wilson Street looking North East.

Above:
The magnificent backdrop behind Ken Payne's garden railway could well be the Peak District, the essential spirit of the Midland. Class 3F 0-6-0 brings a mineral train over Ken's fine viaduct.

Ken Payne's superb Midland Railway. A train of clerestory stock is seen through the archway, with a gleaming Class 2P 4-4-0 at the head. What atmosphere!

Above:
Could this be approaching Buxton? Once again, Ken Payne has captured the full flavour of the Midland Railway in this fine train of crimson coaches hauled by a Black Five. This surely is modelling of a remarkable standard!

Below:
If you know your Ireland, especially in the days when narrow gauge lines wound their leisurely ways over the countryside, you will smell the peat bogs so magnificently captured in this scene on the Kerry Bridge exhibition layout of the Hull M.R.C. Note the man fishing from the pier, his crate of Guinness ready to hand. He is officially in charge of the siding, but that closed 30 years ago!

High Moor station with the Sentinel steam railcar in the bay.

Right – Ravensmoor Queen Street station, Roman Wall junction in the foreground.

Soon after leaving Wilson Street, the line enters another cutting before passing under High Moor, which acts not only as a visual barrier between Hartwich section and Ravensmoor, but is supposed to represent a considerable distance. Once into that tunnel a train is lost to sight and sound, and is presumed to be on a long journey northwards. Emerging from High Moor tunnel, the line immediately runs into a small wayside halt comprising a single island platform, one face served by the main line and the other forming a bay. No main line trains – not even stopping passenger trains – normally call here, except for the one or two trains daily which ply between Ravensmoor and Hartwich Central; usually short two-car trains headed by a tank engine. There is, however, a thrice-daily Sentinel rail-car which provides a shuttle service between High Moor and Ravensmoor, conveying children from the lonely moorland village to Ravensmoor Grammar School and market shoppers to the city.

The line from the bay runs alongside the main line, connected by a crossover just north of High Moor station, and gradually, as Ravensmoor is approached, the lines fan out towards the throat of the terminus. The left-hand line – ie the one from the bay at High Moor – leads to a facing turnout, Roman Wall Junction, where the so-called link-line leads back to Crewchester, thus forming that essential continuous circuit, so useful for testing purposes. It is sometimes used as a running route for trains, both passenger and goods, bound for Hartwich Central, and coming from Port Trenton. It is not however a recognised route between Crewchester Junction and Hartwich Wilson Street. Ravensmoor itself is quite the most ambitious station on the line, with six platforms, a three-road goods depot and a four-road Locomotive shed. Try how I may, I could not find sufficient room for a turntable at Ravensmoor, and as this poses an inevitable question, the question had better be answered here and now.

Engines which have to be turned are driven out of the station and run southwards to a triangle where they are turned before coming back to Ravensmoor shed; that is the fiction! The fact is that they move to that line leading to High Moor bay platform to a spot just beyond Roman Wall junction. Ravensmoor operator informs Crewchester that he has an engine for turning, and then throws the points at Roman Wall Junction to the link-line, thereby automatically transferring power to Crewchester section. As soon as he has a clear path, Crewchester brings the engine on to the triangle at the Junction, turns the engine and sends it back to Ravensmoor. When he is ready, Ravensmoor restores the junction at Roman Wall to 'normal', assuming full control of the engine once again. It sounds complicated; in fact it is simplicity itself, and it works.

For some years, while the line was being built from Trenton to Ravensmoor, Trenton Town in the garage acted as the southern-most terminus of the line, for the extension southwards to London lay somewhere in the future. As Trenton Town was designed for local trains, the two main bay platforms will hold only a maximum of four coaches plus engine if they are not to foul the approach points. Platform 1, the through-road to Port Trenton, will hold a full-length express, but when the line was completed, the only such trains running down the branch were the boat trains for Port Trenton, which do not call at the Town station. There is a short bay platform against the wall of the garage which is used exclusively by the push-pull train running between Trenton and Crewchester Junction, connecting with all main line trains.

Ravensmoor locomotive shed with LNER B12 class 4-6-0 and
Claud *4-4-0 No. 8787 being prepared for the road.*

While all this building was going on, the clockwork engines I had kept were going through Barrie Walls' hands at a most pleasing rate. From the early 1920s up until after the World War II, Bonds produced an 0-6-0ST which became extremely popular among Gauge 0 modellers. They marketed it under the name of BONZONE (corruption of Bonds' Own, I suppose). The J39 and the little Bonzone saddle-tank, *Norah* were the first back, followed by the Tilbury Tank, and then a stream of other engines:- *Edward Thompson*, the A2/3, the 'Precursor' tank, the Parley J3 0-6-0, the Stanier 2-6-4T, the LNER B12/3, the Fowler 4F etc.

The Black Five went to Bob Lovell at his own request as he wanted that clockwork mechanism which he had designed and which so nobly acquitted itself that day at Keen House. Barrie Walls, however added cab-fittings and brake-gear. The other little Bonzone saddle-tank from the Pulham collection, which was a half-cab, presented Barrie with a golden opportunity to fit a full set of working cab details, including hand-brake, regulator, reversing lever, opening firebox door together with a red-glowing fire whenever the engine was in motion! Boxes full of coach bogies came back, insulated with tufnol sleeves which housed the split axles, all these being the standard coned profile cast-iron wheels turned by Bob Lovell in clockwork days.

One of the big questions from the outset had been which motor to adopt, and here I sought advice from fellow-members of the Gauge 0 Guild. It was Walter Mayhew who summarised it best by pointing out the following considerations:

1. My entire layout was level.
2. Ruling curves and points had a radii of 8ft.
3. All coaching stock was running in PTFE bearings, which meant that engines, having once overcome initial inertia from a standing start, were running virtually 'light engine'.

In such circumstances, Wally argued, the little JH motor would be ideal, for no great load was to be imposed upon it; it would be powerful enough for the biggest engines and small enough to fit into the confined space available in small tank engines. Another Walter – Wally West, advised me to fit Muffett gears to all engines, saying that although they were very expensive, once fitted, they would last a life-time.

Here, once again, I must digress to explain the history of the JH motor. When John Hart started practising as a model engineer, he was greatly impressed by the Reid-Maxwell motor, which he considered to be of sound design. He developed the basic principles of this motor, and marketed it under the name 'RM' motor, to which I have alluded several times and which he built entirely by hand on his work-bench in Surbiton. This motor became by general consensus arguably the best and most reliable Gauge 0 motor on the market, but be that as it may, John could never keep up with demand. As I travel round the country meeting other Gauge 0 modellers I hear many a tribute to John and his RM motor. During the 1970s however, John ran into difficulties in that

Two views of Ravensmoor, from the south end box and looking south towards High Moor tunnel.

the firm which supplied magnets and pole-pieces suddenly demanded minimum orders of thousands, thereby placing them beyond John's pocket; the RM motor ground to a halt. One door closes – another opens. A friend of John's, Glen Tyzack (agent for a German-made range of very superior electric motors), showed John one of these motors which he thought might be adapted for Gauge 0. It was impressive, hauling huge loads at about 0.10 amp at 12 volts dc. Thus was born the 'Crailcrest' motor, but John did not possess sole rights on this product, and although he did use it for many of his models, and with great success, he began to hear the cry from model-builders that it was too large to fit into small engines. John went back to his drawing-board and drew up a modified version of the Crailcrest, but with flattened sides enabling it to fit easily into narrow engines.

He demonstrated one of these to me in his workshop, but had no idea of how to go about obtaining sole rights to market it. Together we discussed it with the result that he got Glen Tyzack to agree to manufacture a thousand of the pattern, John to purchase the first five hundred with an option on the rest, and to retain sole rights for two years at least. The motor was an instant success and John was able to repay the bank loan well in advance of the agreed date. Unhappily he died before the full benefits of this motor could be felt, and in any case, he was no business man; he would do anything to avoid picking up a pen! This, then, was the motor I chose for all Crewchester locomotives, a decision I have never had cause to regret.

THE GAUGE 0 GUILD SLIDE SCHEME

The early days of the Guild slide/cassette collection were easy; only three programmes to distribute, and the journeys to photograph other layouts had not yet gathered momentum. However, that momentum was not long in coming, and it is at this point I am faced with an almost insoluble dilemma; which railways to include in these digressions, and which to omit. Every one of them, almost without exception, is of great interest and well worth describing, but unless this book is to take on the characteristics of a mere catalogue, some effort must be made to narrow the selection down, and in so doing there is a very real risk of offending those who will wonder "Why on earh does he not mention so-and-so, a superb layout and one which surely should have been included!" To those people I offer my apologies, but my choice must be guided by as much variety as is possible within these pages. To attempt, for instance, to describe four or five superlative LNER layouts, however fine they may be, would become wearisome and repetitive.

The name of Geoff Pember has become almost a legend in his lifetime as a man who builds models of quite incredible accuracy, to the point where he is not content to use the usual rivetting tool to obtain this effect, but instead used entymological pins which he passes through the body of a loco, soldering them on the inside, thus forming a true rivet. In the Guild programme which I made in the early days of the collection, Geoff tells a story which illustrated his insistence on accuracy. He had built a LNWR locomotive which had inside motion and, as was usual, Geoff had included the inside valve gear in his model, although it would never be seen. Having completed the chassis and motion he laid the chassis on his workbench, and continued with the body. He was visited by Geoff Platt, a keen LNWR expert, who saw and admired the beautiful workmanship of the chassis and motion, but then went on to point out that a mistake had been made in assembling the motion. "You have put right-hand lead in the motion?" Platt told him. "Well, that is normal practice, isn't it?" Pember replied, yet knowing that Platt was something of an authority on LNWR matters. And so he was. Platt went on to explain that Webb gave all his engines left hand-lead, and, as Geoff Pember admits, Platt was correct.

For weeks Geoff Pember pondered the situation which was briefly this: not one in a hundred people who saw the locomotive would even see the inside motion. Of the few who might pick it up and peer inside, how many would know this curious fact that Webb used the more unusual lead for his engines? So was it really worth going to the highly risky trouble of cutting right through the crank axle and trying to reassemble it so as to run true? For months, Geoff said, he agonised over it until finally, using a jeweller's vice and saw, he cut through that crank axle, and by the grace of Heaven it came together true. "The moral of the tale" he says "is that if you are going to build a model – build it correctly in every detail."

While I was with Geoff Pember, I photographed the chassis of a GER 'single', the wheels looking like fine fan tracery in their delicate perfection. He told me that he had lent it to someone to show at an exhibition, and it had been returned to him, packed up in the most slovenly manner so that the chassis was wrecked. Such unforgivable behaviour is rare in our hobby but it does exist. There are people who seem to imagine that model railways come in cardboard boxes, are laid out for a running session, and then put away in the boot cupboard – and if that might appear to be exaggeration, let me cite the gentleman who came to Crewchester one spring day and asked me if I would bring my railway to the Suffolk Show. Checking that the date was not April 1st, I looked at him to see if he were joking, but he was not. I pointed to the railway running right round the garden and asked him "Are you seriously suggesting that I bring all this to your show – ground and set it up there?" "Oh yes" he reassured me "there will be plenty of room, and we will provide some help. And don't worry about transport – we will provide that also."

Possibly one of the best known Gauge 0 garden railways is that of Don Neale, whose Kirtley branch includes quite the most magnificent viaduct, spanning the width of the garden, that I have ever seen. Even people who cannot remember the name of Neale know exactly who I mean when I say something about the garden railway with the fine viaduct, and as I travel about the country, photographing all sorts of layouts, it is quite remarkable how many modellers refer to Don Neale, saying that it was his railway which inspired them. He was one of that small band of Gauge 0 enthusiasts who gathered in 1956 to try to form what became the Gauge 0 Guild, after which event we would meet at the AGM at Keen House. But my first visit to Don's home was on the day of the Royal Wedding of Prince Charles and Princess 'Di', a lovely summer day when the garden was looking at its best. Don himself, who was in the local Fire Service, had been on duty all night, yet he stayed up all day with me so that we might make a Guild programme on his railway. The garden was looking at its best, tended by Joan, his wife, and the railway was regarded by both as an integral part of the garden: therefore both railway and garden must be kept to the highest possible standards – a mutually agreed policy. Don is also the author of a standard book on garden railways, his own garden line bearing witness to his qualifications.

Having a garden railway of my own, it is not unnatural that I should feel a rather special affinity for outdoor railways. While it is true that in such a capricious climate as ours there is much to be said for indoor layouts, but to my mind the disadvantages of the outdoor layout are far outweighed by the benefits. Quite apart from the scenic effects obtainable in the garden, there is the question of lighting. No artificial light can replace the ambience of daylight. Then there is the considerable factor of perspective, for out in the garden, where no painted backdrop is necessary, it does not matter from what angle one observes the line, the perspective is right.

Another railway which has fascinated me from the moment I first saw it was Ken Payne's outdoor layout. For very good reasons Ken has had to dismantle the garden railway and build another indoors, but the setting of that original layout was one of the most spectacular I have ever seen. Living in a remote valley, Ken's home lay on a hillside in the sort of scenery one usually finds on picture postcards. I once asked him if he really appreciated how fortunate he was to live in such a place, and his reply was "Jack – I've lived here for fifteen years and still sometimes pinch myself; nothing would make me leave it." Evidence of this sincerity was shown when he was offered work which would bring him a vastly increased income, provided he was prepared to move. He rejected it. Staying there one night in 1988, I woke in the morning to look out of the bedroom window on the perfect English scene – rolling, tree-girt hillsides and a gentle valley through which flowed a stream. This is not as irrelevant as it may seem, for it was that very scene which formed the natural backdrop to that outdoor layout. His Midland Railway layout could have been in the Peak District. As I have said, for purely practical considerations the railway in the garden has had to be moved indoors, into a purpose-built stone building, and the highest compliment I can pay Ken is that the present layout is better than the first. Ken's railway is one of the very finest quality, the track and models being fine-scale and super-detailed, but in sharp contrast is yet another most remarkable model railway which I photographed about the same time. The contrast lay in the fact that whereas Ken's railway was fine-scale, Vic Martin's was anything but fine-scale, yet it was unique in my experience.

I first heard of Vic's railway through a letter he wrote me, in which he wondered whether his line might be worth a visit. 3000 feet of track and over 50 trains, all operated to timetable and covering a vast area, seemed to be to me a reasonable pretext for driving down to the Isle of Sheppey in Kent to find the secluded house. Having been misdirected once or twice I at last found the grassy track leading to the house, where the door-bell was in the form of a plunger-type block-bell. I rang "Call attention" (one bell) and the door was opened by a man dressed in an LMS porter's uniform. Suddenly I realised that I had seen this man before on television, together with his wife, also dressed in railway uniform. It had been a programme like 'Woman's Hour', and the whole subject of their model railway was treated in an unbearably patronising manner, the interviewer being a lady with a cut-glass BBC voice who patently did not understand what she was seeing. Thinly veiled fun was poked at the LMS uniforms and one or two quite inexcusable jibes were made at this juvenile hobby, being indulged in by two grown adults. I remember being angry when I saw the programme, and now here I was, face to face with one of the victims.

Vic Martin, well into his seventies when I met him, was a fascinating character: local historian, landowner, engineer, naturalist, and railway enthusiast. His house, which had been built with his own hands, was crammed with objects of railway interest, which he showed me with relish. I was introduced to Louie, his wife, who was suffering from the cruel malady which ultimately led to her death, and who was a highly intelligent lady, but as the daughter of the one-time signals and telegraph manager at St Pancras station had forgotten more about railway procedure than most of us ever learn. Every day they would work a session on their railway, Vic at the main station, Warden Point, and Louie at the subsidiary box at Swale Tunnel. A variety of animals roamed their garden and the adjacent fields, all belonging to Vic, and every time I visited these two delightful people I would go round with Vic, feeding this miniature zoo.

There were full-size signals in the grounds of the house, where the lamps were lit at night (a practice ridiculed by the TV interviewer), and all round the field was what I can only describe as a system of trunking, similar to the sort of air-conditioning conduits one sees on factory walls, but laid on their sides here and mounted on sections of telegraph poles up to about table-top height. I was told that these tightly sealed units contained the railway, and I did begin to wonder just how I was going to make a Guild programme on a labyrinth of metal-covered pipes. I was then led to a long shed, some 80 feet in length, approached via an outbuilding in which I saw a great array of accumulators, reminding me of Stanley Norris. Here was the source of power supply. Inside the shed lay the visible section of the railway, a mass of parallel tracks, forests of semaphore signals, all with their coloured lights, and countless repeater signals suspended on the wall, with a control-panel up at the far end of the room. Here lay not only the complicated control-panel for the entire layout, with full track-circuited and illuminated track diagrams, and a battery of block instruments. Behind the operator's seat hung a sheaf of documents which were the actual full working timetable out of St Pancras in 1930. The engines were all home-made by Vic, not – as he put it – to exhibition standards, but acceptable representations of their prototype.

At one end of the room the lines plunged into Duke of Clarence tunnel and then on to St Pancras (out of sight), while the other end of the shed held Swale Tunnel Junction station which stood at the mouth of yet another tunnel leading out into the field and all those tubes. Every inch of track, all wiring, and all the electrical gadgetry was the handiwork of this amazing man, and at nearly eighty years of age he was able to operate that entire system single-handed if need be. (Louie was often unfit to join in.)

Vic Martin's Warden Point North station looking towards Duke of Clarence tunnel and St. Pancras.

But the most dramatic surprise was yet to come. Taking his seat at the controls, while Louie, now dressed in her LMS uniform took over at Swale, Vic said to me "I'm afraid I shan't be able to talk to you while the trains are running, Jack; it gets a bit complicated." Apparently the practice was to run the full 24-hour cycle of the timetable, night-time working offering some respite to the operators, and peak-hours doing just the reverse. At the end of each session the clocks would be stopped, and the timetable resumed at the next session, with seldom a day being missed. I settled down to watch, Clarence tunnel to my right, and Swale to my left. Right down into Duke of Clarence tunnel I could see the winking signal lights, and the slightly darkened room gave a wonderful effect. I heard Vic ringing the 'opening box' signal on his block bell "Five-five-five", answered by Louie from Swale, and then Louie's voice on the intercom calling "Four-forty and ticking!" This meant that the clocks had been re-started at 4.40pm.

Now here I must explain that the 80-foot stretch of visible track before me was meant to represent a section of main line on the LMS (ex-Midland) somewhere between Hendon and Elstree, the very line on which I had travelled daily for five years between Hendon and Kentish Town in my schooldays. After a while I heard Vic offer a stopping passenger train to Louie ('Three-one') and I put my head down almost level with the track to see what would emerge from Duke of Clarence tunnel. Then I suddenly realised that the clock had moved on to just after 5pm and that the train I was about to see would be my school train from fifty years ago – the 4.45 off St Pancras, 4.51 off Kentish Town and arriving at Hendon at 5.09 before continuing all stations to St Albans. In 1930 that train would be an eight-car set of 1923 compartment stock headed by a 2-6-4T.

I became stupidly excited as I heard a distant rumbling from the tunnel, and then from its portals came – – a 2-6-4T with eight LMS compartment coaches! Immediately my mind went back to those schooldays, and I remembered that round about the time my train drew into Hendon, an up express, usually hauled by a compound, would come racing through on the up fast road. Hardly had the recollection formed in my mind than I heard a train in Swale Tunnel – and from it burst a long train of corridor coaches headed by a 'crimson rambler' – a Midland compound, which raced along the line until it was swallowed up in Clarence tunnel. From then on, I was walking on air, for every train was as real to me as if I had returned to my boyhood and was once again travelling on that line. I made up my mind there and then that I would make such a Guild programme on this railway for the Guild as would set the record straight about this likeable couple and their magnificent railway and although it entailed a 250 mile round trip, I went back on a number of occasions.

The railway was truly amazing. A train which was seen on its way to Glasgow would not be seen again for several days, spending the time out in the middle of that field, secure in the weatherproof trunking. Track-circuiting, train annunciators, every device was there to inform Vic exactly where every train was. Not only did the trains run from St Pancras, but goods trains would work through from places such as Eltham on the Southern, via the North London loop. I have seen finer models, more detailed station buildings and more immaculate control-panels, but never have I seen a more realistically run system, with the possible exception perhaps of Ken Longbottom's Diggle and Westport, nor on such a vast scale.

When eventually I had completed the programme on that railway I took it down to Sheppey to show Louie and Vic, so that they could add the commentary. At the end of the programme, while we were still recording, Vic sprung a surprise on me by saying "Well Jack, we feel that you have really given a true account of our railway, and because you live so far away we know you cannot become a regular operator, but we would like to make you an honorary Director of the railway, and Louie will give you your Director's pass." Could any man ask for a better reward for his efforts! At one point in the interview I had asked Vic about this LMS uniform business, and that I had heard remarks by people to the effect that Vic and Louie must be slightly crazy to go that far.

"Well," Vic replied "when the LMS became BR they had a whole lot of surplus LMS porters' uniforms which they were selling off at ten bob (50p) each, so we bought a few. When you go to play cricket you wear flannels; when you play football you wear shorts, so when you play trains what is so daft about wearing railway uniform? Besides," he added, "for twenty years I haven't bought any working clothes at all, so who's crazy?" I will personally vouch for the sanity of these two very warm-hearted, hospitable, and kindly people.

By the end of 1981, thirty Guild programmes had been completed and were in circulation, some of them completed only a short while before the owners' death, reminding us that there was no time to be lost if some permanent record of these fine model railways was to be preserved for the archives. Of those thirty programmes completed during the first two years of the scheme, the names of eight of them have now passed into history.

Among this roll of honour stands another name which will be known to many people – R. E. Tustin, author of what was for many years considered to be the standard work on garden railways. I first met Ray Tustin during the very early days of the Guild slide/cassette scheme whilst making a programme on the garden railway of Martin Bloxsom in Leicestershire. Martin Bloxsom, a schoolmaster, was another of the many disciples of John Hart, and in fact I was staying with him when the news of John's sudden death came through. Like both John and myself, Martin ran his stud-contact railway with the help of a bunch of enthusiastic youngsters, so I was quite accustomed to seeing the garden dotted with people whom I did not know. One afternoon Martin took me down the garden to meet a man who was standing by one of the stations, saying, ''Jack, I would like you to meet Ray Tustin''; up to that moment I had no idea that Ray was a near neighbour of Martin's. I knew the name R. E. Tustin of course but to meet him was to come face to face with yet another legend in his lifetime.

We met on a number of occasions and perhaps one of the most treasured memories of those days was when at the Lutterworth Model Railway Society's annual convention, Ray and I sat together on a panel, the subject being, not surprisingly, garden railways. Scheduled to run for perhaps thirty minutes or so (a sort of open forum for questions on garden layouts), after one and a half hours, the meeting had to be brought to a close as the lecture hall was required for another function, so keenly interested were the audience. Ray was a quiet man, his soft voice never raised and his manner unruffled and calm, yet his authority was clear for all to see. My own contributions that afternoon were small, for I should have been sitting in the body of the hall, but I learned much by just listening to his gentle, almost tentative replies to questions.

One day Martin told me of something which he thought might warrant one of my Guild slide programmes – a product of Ray Tustin's clever hands and mind. Ray, now well into his seventies, had as a young man lived in Hampton Wick on the Thames, and as a diversion from model railway building had made a complete diorama of Hampton Wick High Street as it was in his young days. Having been closely concerned with town-planning in that area, he had access to many official sources, plans and maps. So, coupled with his own engineering skill and artistic flair, he had all the ingredients of a highly authentic scene. In due course a day was agreed upon and I went to Ray's house where the Hampton Wick High Street diorama had been set up for me to photograph. It was one of the most beautifully executed miniatures I have ever seen, with vehicles of all kinds representing the 1920s, 1930s and 1940s, including every conceivable type of bus and tram, all built to 7mm scale. Every shop was faithfully reproduced in full detail, and, being familiar with the street myself, I could recognise some of the buildings which are still there today. But the amazing thing to me was when Ray told me that not one single transfer had been used anywhere on the diorama – every letter, sign, poster, etc. had been hand-painted by Ray himself.

The piece-de-resistance, which Ray kept until last, was a circus train – a travelling fair. To anyone interested in London's transport, Ray's commentary is an encyclopaedia of history. I do not know what has happened to that little gem of a diorama, but at least it has been preserved on film for all to see and enjoy – and wonder at the affectionate care and skill which had gone into its making. The whole thing – the model itself, with Ray's gentle voice – do give a very real picture of the man himself. He is sadly missed.

During these first two years of the Guild slide collection I met a number of people who had been very little more than well-known names hitherto, such as Geoff Bigmore. His layout, Bigston, is well-known to almost every railway modeller for it has been running, and has appeared in articles in the model press, for well over a quarter of a century; but I had met Geoff only casually at the Easter show on one or two occasions. But now I had arranged to spend a day with him at his home in order to make a Guild programme on the line.

Railway modellers, like all humanity, are a mixture of sharp contrasts, ranging from the quiet gentleness of Ray Tustin to the mercurial temperature of Martin Bloxsom who has a mind which seems to be something between greased lightning and a heart-attack. Geoff Bigmore was one of the quiet men, his lean, thoughtful face and slightly shy manner concealing considerable knowledge, no little modelling skill, and warm affection for his hobby. His railway ran from a shed at the top (house) end of the sloping garden down to a further shed at the bottom, the line on a falling gradient which did not match the slope of the ground, so that by the time one reached the bottom shed, the line was almost shoulder high, whereas at the top it was barely eighteen inches above ground level. Several impressions remain vivid in my memory of that day not least – the somersault signals (GNR) – for anyone with any experience of building semaphores knows the problems posed by the somersault arm – and a stunning rake of twelve North London four-wheeled coaches. Most modellers are content to make one of such a vehicle, or perhaps a set of three, but to build twelve perfectly matching coaches of such high quality takes a kind of dedication and care which must be rare.

When it came to recording the spoken commentary, Geoff's shyness showed itself, and he admitted to me that this was the part he had dreaded – ''I'm not awfully good at speaking, Jack.'' We retired to a quiet room, I set up my recording gear and microphones, and within thirty minutes had recorded the perfect tape – without once having to stop and re-record a word or sentence. In my experience this is extremely rare and has happened only once or twice throughout the whole time I have been running the scheme. When I started to dismantle the equipment Geoff looked up in some puzzlement. ''Is that it, then, Jack?'' I told him that it was indeed 'it' and that I had never been given such an easy passage by a layout owner. He looked quite surprised and said ''Good heavens – and I was dreading this part! And that's all there is to it?''

A week or so later he phoned me, telling me that his old friend, Norman Eagles had been on the line to him asking if Jack Ray had been to see him. When Geoff told him that I had indeed been there, Norman said ''Well, Jack is due here next Friday, and although I know him, I am a bit worried about this recording business. How did you get on with that bit?'' Geoff chuckled as he told me: ''I told Norman 'It's a piece of cake – there is nothing to it; you just sit and chat to Jack, that's all.' He seemed relieved.'' Neither Geoff nor Norman are still with us, yet thanks to their hospitality and cooperation, it is still possible to see their railways and hear their voices enthusing about the hobby just as if one were standing beside them in their own homes.

In 1951 there occurred the Festival of Britain, for which post-war celebration, Derby Museum planned a model railway layout depicting every phase of Midland Railway history, with a whole room in the museum being devoted to this project, planned to last about ten years. I had paid fleeting visits to this superlative model railway on my way to the north, but had never seen it working, so I wrote to the Principal Keeper of Derby Museum asking if it might be possible for me to come and make a Guild programme on the layout – now thirty years old – before the threatened dismantling and transfer to another building took place. I received a most cordial reply inviting me to come and spend a day at the museum when the railway room would be put at my disposal. Further, this gentleman, Mr R. G. Hughes, had arranged for two 'friends of the railway', Alan Doig and his assistant, Tim Flint, to be with me all day and operate the trains.

When I arrived at the museum it was obvious that parking was going to be a problem, for I had a lot of heavy gear to transport to the railway room, but even that had been taken care of by the thoughtful Mr Hughes. A uniformed attendant appeared from nowhere, unlocked a barrier and ushered me on to a reserved space right beside a side-entrance which was close by the railway room. Arthur Dewar had come along with me to lend a hand and with Alan Doig and Tim Flint to help, we were very quickly at work. The railway was extensive, to say the least, and was enclosed in glass all along the public side, making serious problems of reflection of light for the photographer, but nothing was too much trouble for these men of goodwill.

Crawling through trap-door, and propelling myself along the floor under the complicated baseboards on a little flat trolley, lying flat on my stomach, I was guided like some troglodite visitor to certain places where a trap-door could be opened in the scenery and one could pop up to obtain unrivalled viewpoints of the railway. However, adequate as these vantage-points may be for normal maintenance jobs, they were slightly less than generous for an ageing man with tripods, cameras, floodlamps etc. Every item of rolling stock and every engine, all in historical chronological order was brought up for my camera, so that I felt like a small boy who had been let loose with carte blanche in a sweet-shop. Alan and Tim had given up their day off to perform all this work, a task of some magnitude, for it entailed fetching out items which were not normally on view to the public; this in turn demanding physical contortions of an often painful nature as Tim crawled and writhed among the cables, supporting uprights and interweaving baseboards. The cheerful badinage between these two men must have disguised many a suppressed oath or curse. When the job was finished, Alan Doig told me that I really ought now to go to Matlock museum, for, he told me, they have started where we finished off!

So it was that I wrote to David White of Slaters, who was responsible for the two huge Midland Railway dioramas in the Matlock Railway Museum. Once again I was assisted by Arthur Dewar, and when we saw that exhibition we were astonished; in fact it is difficult to find words for the railway without running out of superlatives. The first and smaller diorama depicted Monsal Dale viaduct in its heyday with all the dramatic scenery of the Peak District, and the second diorama is of Millers Dale station and the two great steel viaducts which span road and river there. The glass panels were thrown back so that I, in stockinged feet, might walk over the river-bed and obtain views which would have been impossible to the normal visitor. David White gave up most of his day to guide me round and help in selecting shots, after which he

made the recorded commentary. Another Martin Bloxham is David – with a mind that races and a voice to match; a veritable powerhouse of human energy.

Barrie Walls has already appeared in these pages, but only as a benefactor to Crewchester; nothing has been said about his own very fine exhibition railway, based upon Great Eastern practice, running into LNER days, and depicting the East Anglian scene. Barrie, with his 'trade-mark' woolly hat and his friendly smile, together with Rosie, his wife (who, I suspect, knows just about as much about operating a model railway as Barrie himself!) and his two sons are popular and familiar figures at exhibitions. Unlike most modellers, Barrie does not have to rely on suspect scale drawings of locomotives, for he has serviced these engines and knows more about what they really looked like and how they worked than the most enthusiastic dilettante modeller. When he builds a GE engine he already knows every nut, bolt, rod, valve and lever of the prototype, and on one or two occasions, while building or modifying a model for me, he has corrected the official drawing in some detail – from memory. His own fine-scale railway is a joy to behold, and is run in truly authentic manner; yet it is typical of the man that when I presented him with the task of converting my ancient, over-scale J3 built by Rev. Parley, Barrie set to it with zest, adding brake gear, full cab-detail, and so on. There was not the slightest suggestion that this crude bit of railway pre-history was beneath him – it was a model locomotive and that was enough for Barrie, and from that sow's ear he produced, if not a silk purse, at least an engine which still gives me a lot of pleasure, not least by reasons of its provenance.

Another stronghold penetrated by relatively few privileged visitors was the Bromford and High Peak Railway owned by the late Colonel Ronnie Hoare. Having gone through the necessary protocol, I eventually received an invitation to spend two days in Poole, making a Guild programme on this famous railway. The Colonel was out of the country at the time, but I was shepherded by the late Hugh Joslyn, who also did the commentary.

Bromford and High Peak is a rich man's railway, everything being of the finest obtainable quality, with people such as Vic Green, Stanley Beeson, and Bernard Miller being responsible for the vast majority of the models. Following that first visit I received a letter from Colonel Hoare regretting that he was unable to be present when I came to the railway, and asking me to come again, giving him plenty of notice so that he might entertain me personally. In fact I did go back in January 1989 and Ronnie Hoare's interpretation of hospitality is generous in the extreme. Already a very sick man, and confined to a wheel-chair, he insisted on meeting me when I arrived, and not only spent most of the long weekend with me, but arranged for John Maclie to look after me when he was unavailable himself. As he was only recently discharged from hospital after a serious heart-attack, it was only by reason of his indomitable strength of character and kindness of heart which prompted him to spend the better part of three days with me. He was a good listener as well as a fascinating talker, and it was typical of him to arrange a sort of final farewell lunch party at Bournemouth's finest hotel before I left for home.

He insisted on dispensing with the attendant nurse and wheel-chair, plus one of his luxurious cars for a whole day, preferring to travel about in my old banger, chatting as enthusiastically as a school-boy about all manner of things, and as we drove he asked me, almost shyly "I hope you will not be in too much of a hurry to leave on Sunday, Jack?" When I assured him that, provided I could start for home sometime during the afternoon, there was no

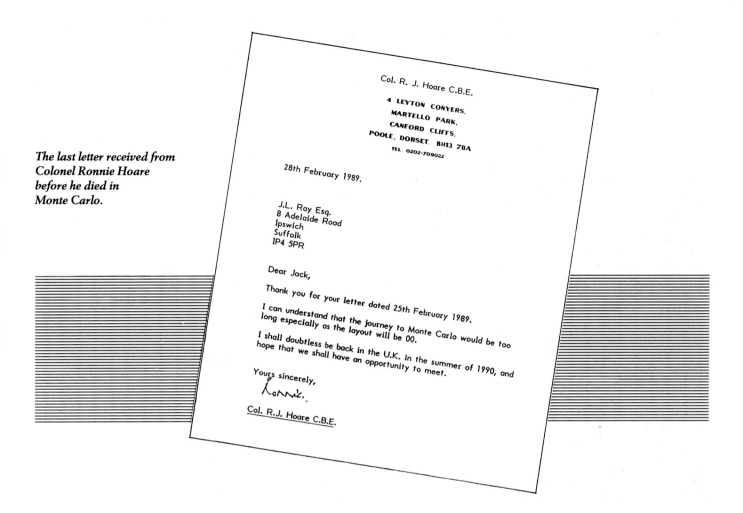

The last letter received from Colonel Ronnie Hoare before he died in Monte Carlo.

Col. R. J. Hoare C.B.E.

4 LEYTON CONYERS,
MARTELLO PARK,
CANFORD CLIFFS,
POOLE, DORSET. BH13 7BA
TEL. 0202-709022

28th February 1989.

J.L. Ray Esq.
8 Adelaide Road
Ipswich
Suffolk
IP4 5PR

Dear Jack,

Thank you for your letter dated 25th February 1989.

I can understand that the journey to Monte Carlo would be too long especially as the layout will be 00.

I shall doubtless be back in the U.K. in the summer of 1990, and hope that we shall have an opportunity to meet.

Yours sincerely,

Ronnie.

Col. R.J. Hoare C.B.E.

immediate panic, he said "Well – I have asked Stanley Beeson and his wife to join us for lunch – I hope that is all right?"

That weekend held another amusing incident. On my way to lunch on Sunday I wanted to buy some flowers for the lady of the house, but there was no florist open in Bournemouth on a Sunday, so I made for the biggest garage-filling-station I could find, where the usual flowers were on sale – hardly what I had wanted, and far from a respectable bouquet. But it was better than arriving empty-handed, so I ordered a half-a-dozen bunches. While these were being put together by the attendant, I happened to glance up at the name of the garage – and it read "R. J. HOARE ASSOCIATES"!

I am glad now that I made the journey, for Colonel Hoare himself made the recorded commentary on the revised programme and that voice may still be heard. He did invite me to Monte Carlo a few weeks later, but I think even then he knew his time was limited for he died in July 1989 and I never made that trip. The reason for the projected visit was to make a programme on a new 00 layout he had recently bought, and about which he was as enthusiastic as a boy with his first train-set!

There is a rather pleasant postscript to my association with Colonel Ronnie Hoare which I think is worth recording. Many of the locomotives in his collection were built by Vic Green, a man whom I had never met, and not really heard of. During my last visit to Hoare, on a day which we spent on the railway, he told me that he had quite a number of engines on order, some of them in fact on test on his railway, before being completed and painted. All were

being built by Vic Green. Now, despite the fact that we had never actually met, I had corresponded with Vic, and after Hoare's death that correspondence intensified to the point where a 'pen-friend-ship' developed. Vic turned out to be a fascinating correspondent with a highly entertaining style of writing, as anyone who has read his articles will know, and I have, through that correspondence, been able to catch glimpses of what is involved in model-making of such quality. Before even cutting the first piece of metal or turning the first wheel, Vic will carry out research involving visits to anywhere where an extant example of the prototype can be found, or if not – its next-of-kin. Books and works drawings will be secured or bought, and having worked for the Board of British Rail, he has contacts beyond the reach of most of us, and even during the building of the model, Vic will go back to that shed to re-examine or check some detail. This involves expenditure of a sum exceeding that which most of us would be prepared to pay for the completed model, and only the very wealthy can find that sort of money.

When Ronnie Hoare died, a considerable list of orders were outstanding with Vic Green, upon which he had already started work and spent much money – with no guarantee now that these could be sold. Shortly after his death, a party of people involved in handling the Colonel's affairs called upon Vic, asked for a full list of outstanding orders, and then drew up a document to ensure that the contract would be fulfilled, taking over ten years. This, they said, just to keep the name of Ronnie Hoare bright and shining!

THE NEW 12-VOLT, TWO RAIL SYSTEM
– THE OLD ORDER PASSETH –

The decade of the 1980s had started with upheaval, involving retirement, the new Crewchester Railway, and the Guild slide/cassette scheme, but by 1983 the new pattern of life had established itself into a comfortable – if sometimes strenuous – pattern. With John Hart no longer there to help out with problems, I felt like the trainee pilot now told he must fly solo. The Guild members who had rallied round me when I went two-rail continued to be supportive and I was not lacking in friends; but when one reaches that time in life when one's contemporaries begin to disappear from the scene, old friends become even more important. So it was that Arthur Dewar and I spent two enjoyable holidays in Mull and Skye, as well as the mainland where once the three of us – Arthur, John Hart and I – had enjoyed a memorable holiday.

Mention has already been made of the rapid sociological changes of the past few years and their effect upon Crewchester, but there came a time in the early 1980s when these changes came home to me in an almost bewildering manner. For almost 30 years I had had no difficulty in recruiting boys of thirteen years of age and upwards who either had model railways of their own or were to some degree interested in railways: simply put up a notice in the local Secondary and Grammar schools, and along would come my applicants. Always, these lads had some basic knowledge of and understanding of what railways were about; all I had to do was teach them some of the finer points of block signalling, marshalling and operating trains to timetables &c., and within a year or so they would become sufficiently competent to run the entire system. But times were changing. Six youngsters came to see what it was all about; they were all about thirteen, and varied from obvious 'University material' to the late-developer. They were well-mannered lads and paid keen attention to my explanations of how Crewchester was run. They saw cine films, slides, and were encouraged to go outside when the weather was fine and just 'play trains' by driving an engine up and down a few sidings.

There was no point in hurrying things. I had always found in the past that it was best to give them something to *do* and let them get the feel of the railway before pumping a lot of technical stuff into them. Then came the first shock. Not one of those lads knew how points worked or could determine which road was set when they were switched. None of them knew what a tank engine was, or why one did not have to turn it on the turntable. None could distinguish between compartment stock and corridor stock. And why in heaven's name should they?(!) Not one of them had (a) ever travelled in a train or even (b) stood on a railway station. The horrors of the deprived lives of the youngsters of today came home to me as a great shock. Give them a computer and they would make it sit up and beg. Show them a TV set and they would service it for you. But ask them to set the road for a train coming into platform 1 ("What's platform One, Mr Ray?") and they looked at me in blank incomprehension. Admittedly it was a bad summer and many a weekend would see us rained off; but on other weekends when the sun shone they might fail to turn up because their big sister was getting married and the family were off to the Bahamas for the weekend where she wanted to be married . . . or "Dad's taking us to Portugal for the weekend so I can't come next week."

Patience, Ray! This is a new generation – take your time! But then even more sinister events began to take place. Pick-up goods trains were sent down to Crewchester headed by a Pacific, and no brake-van on the end. It took me ages to explainl that in the olden days, no train of wagons ever moved without its brake van at the tail end. I was regarded as some sort of prehistoric fanatic, and had probably fought in the war with bows and arrows, someone to be humoured, but totally out of touch with the world of today – some truth in that, I dare say! But it did have its lighter side.

One of these young lads was as bright as a button; tell him something once, and it stuck. He picked up the block bell code after one or two sessions, and I was soon able to give him a whole section to work. On one such occasion I was trying to instruct one of the slower lads in the block bells at Ravensmoor, and it was hard going for both of us. The bright lad was working down at Hartwich and slowly and painfully I persuaded my pupil to offer him a stopping passenger train. It took me a good two minutes to get past 'Call attention' but eventually we managed to struggle through to obtaining acceptance of the train from Hartwich, and checking the pegger to 'line clear'. Then came the moment to despatch the train and I waxed eloquent over the vital importance of observing every stage of correct procedure. With trembling hands the lad turned the controller slowly round until the train moved out of the platform and started down the garden towards High Moor tunnel. When the engine reached High Moor tunnel it suddenly jerked to a stop. This was a blow; my clever lad down at Hartwich had forgotten to switch his controller on, so, leaving my pupil, I went down the garden to see what that boy was doing. He was sitting by his controller, happily watching the scene but making no attempt to turn his controller up to receive the train he had accepted on the block instrument. "Come on," I said, "wake up – you've accepted the train on your instrument. Now it is stuck." He smiled happily up at me. "Hullo, Mr Ray. Something wrong, is there?" I should have been warned by that mischievous look, but I ploughed on. "Yes. There is something very much wrong, lad. That stopping passenger train is stuck half in to High Moor tunnel."

"Yes, it would be, wouldn't it Mr Ray. It has gone into my section." "Well, why for Pete's sake don't you turn your controller on, lad?" Another seraphic smile. "I will – when I get two bells from Ravensmoor." I think he rather enjoyed catching old know-all out. In my efforts to coax my pupil through the procedure I had entirely forgotten to give "Train entering section" as it left.

Sadly, those six lads quickly lost interest in the railway, and who shall blame them, for unlike my generation, railways play no part in the lives of today's youngsters. But most weekends at least one other operator would turn up and a two-man session can be most enjoyable; while on other occasions I would be on my own – a far cry from the halcyon days when I was hard put to it to find work for fifteen boys. Nicky Mudd, alone of all the old gang, still comes along almost every weekend, and at times we even have as many as four people, a real luxury; one at Rockhill, one at Crewchester, one at Hartwich and the last at Ravensmoor. But the block bells and instruments are still in the positions they occupied for the old four-track system and are not really ideally disposed for present day working. Another big job for the future!

The mid 1980s brought another unexpected and delightful bonus in the shape of my younger brother, whose health had been severely undermined by his war experiences and various domestic problems. We were brought together again as joint trustees of my late grandfather's estate, and in the fifteen years during which we worked together we rediscovered the comradeship of our boyhood. Alan began to visit Crewchester, and although he was a very sick man, within an hour of arriving, the years would visibly fall away from him, and we would run the railway all day. It was almost as if I had discovered the real reason for building Crewchester, so much pleasure do we derive from it, albeit rarely, for his health presents serious problems in travelling the twelve miles which separate us. And this was not the only good thing to come out of those mid 1980s, for Eddie Bye re-appeared on the scene.

When I first met Eddie at John Hart's house during the late 1950s, he was in his early twenties, and we would meet frequently at Surbiton. A merry man, is Eddie, with a sharp wit and clever hands, for he had sat for years at the feet of John Hart, where he had learned much of John's techniques. He had very quickly shown great skill in painting coaches and locomotives, carrying out the most exquisitely delicate lining and lettering, often commented on by John. Although he had in fact once visited the old clockwork Crewchester he had not been a regular operator, and it was not until after John Hart's death and my subsequent conversion to two-rail that he made the first of what was to be many pilgrimages to Ipswich. Although quick to offer praise where it is due, Eddie is reluctant to criticise the workmanship of others, and his admiration of people like Barrie Walls is always in evidence.

Perhaps the greatest help to me is the honesty and clarity of his appraisal of my own efforts. If he likes something on my railway he will say so without gushing; if there is that which he finds less than acceptable he remains silent, although if pushed he will venture an opinion. Over the years he has made many items of rolling stock for Crewchester, including a four-car set of LMS compartment stock, a five-car set of 1923 main line LMS stock, a Southern PMV, a Southern through-coach (for we both adopt the conceit that our lines are linked), but his masterpiece is the 'Claud Hamilton' which he built for me, just for the fun of attempting the challenge. 'Fun' is hardly the word, for that model fought him every inch of the way, as some things will. Everything that could go wrong did go wrong, but with the aid of much patience and many expletives more associated with Billingsgate than Keen House, he finished the lovely engine, turned her out in LNER apple green, gave her the royal number 8787, and, for good measure included inside working motion. With her fine 7ft driving wheels, the engine is a fit LNER counterpart to the LMS 7ft compound which also runs at Crewchester.

More and more journeys were made over the country with my cameras and tape-recorder as I added to the Guild collection, and in 1984 and 1985 I did two tours of Scotland, making ten new programmes on various club and privately owned railways. It is unthinkable to speak of model railways in Scotland without mentioning one man – Nigel Macmillan, for not only has he built a number of layouts for his own amusement in his own home, but also for public exhibition.

It is my contention that if anything is Scottish, runs on rails and has wheels, Nigel has built a model of it. His own permanent railway in the loft of his Glasgow house (he has two homes – one in Glasgow and one in Aberdeen, for he is liable to be called out at any time of the day or night to be taken out to some accident on an oil rig) has a fine assortment of Scottish railway items as well as a fine selection of authentic models of trams from every city and town in Scotland. He is also the creator of the Gauge 0 exhibition layout known as Lyoncross Colliery, and the Campbeltown and Machrihanish Light Railway (7mm models running on 4mm track).

Both these exhibition layouts are extensive and complex which, when assembled for an exhibition, occupy a considerable area and demand a lot of heavy labour, as will be appreciated by anyone with experience of this sort of activity. Consider then what happened during one of my tours of Scotland! On two successive days, Nigel organised a van for transport, one the first day bringing the entire Lyoncross Colliery layout to the premises of the Renfrewshire Model Railway Club in Elderslie, erecting it, helping me all day in photographing the layout, dismantling it and returning it to its place of storage; on the second day repeating this Herculean task with the Campbeltown and Machrihanish layout – then, for good measure sitting down with me for three hours to make the recorded commentaries! As if this were not good enough, I was invited to make yet another programme on his own loft railway in Glasgow.

Nigel, a staunch Scottish Nationalist of the nicer kind, who, with his son Gordon and his wife Nette, appear on Scottish TV in Highland dancing, has a rather amusing trap for the unwary visiting Sassenach on his home layout. He will mention casually that on this very Scottish model railway he runs a 'Castle'. When the visitor expresses surprise that a Scottish layout should feature a GWR engine, Nigel explains that it is *Cluny Castle*, whereupon some unwary visitors have fallen straight into the trap, pointing out kindly that down in England we pronounce it *Clun Castle*: whereupon Nigel wheels out his beautiful Highland Railway Peter Drummond 4-6-0, *Cluny Castle*!

Scotland is indeed rich in model railways, the Renfrewshire Model Railway Club possessing several of different gauges in their fine premises in Elderslie. This very live club seems to me to be the epitome of such organisations, for they *own* their premises, which are kept in beautiful condition, and there is a give-and-take between the gauges which is rare. Gauge 0, 00, and even smaller gauges all have their adherents, but when one of these factions holds an exhibition, all hands are put to making it a success, abandoning their own preferred medium to ensure that which ever layout is being shown will be seen to the best advantage. When I called there to make a Guild programme, all the club members rallied round to help; I was hardly allowed to lift a tripod for myself, so anxious were these people to make my way easy, and to cap it all, I was served with a lunch which would have done credit to a first-rate hotel – all prepared by club members – not their womenfolk!

Further north, in Aberdeen, I was the guest of Dr. Martin Cheshire, in whose beautiful house was a very fine Gauge 0 layout. The trackwork alone is remarkable, meticulously detailed, and every single one of the hundreds of rail-joints are linked by correct fish-plates, bolted with four 16BA bolts and nuts! When I asked Martin what he did about isolation sections, he grinned and said "What do the banks tell you to do with expired credit cards?"

It is so difficult when speaking of these journeys to make Guild programmes not to embark upon a catalogue of the amazing people and model railways I encounter.

There can surely be few railway modellers (at least those of the older generation) who do not at least know the name Geoffrey Keen; after all, the London headquarters of The Model Railway Club is known as Keen House. During 1986, news reached me that the late Geoffrey Keen's models were to be disposed of very shortly, and could the Gauge 0 Guild do anything to preserve them at least on film before it was too late? It appeared that Mrs Keen, now well into her nineties, and a keen model railway operator in her own right (her railway was known as the Pantry Dockyard Railway!), was now finding it impossible to maintain even what was left of the collection. With no time to lose I wrote to Mrs Keen, seeking permission to come and visit her with a view to making some sort of archives-record of the collection before it was disposed of. Immediately I received a reply that not only would I be welcome, but that she had arranged for John Anning, a close associate of Keen's, to be present when I came. This was a bonus, for although I had seen John Anning at various meetings and exhibitions, we had never had the opportunity to get to know each other.

Geoffrey Keen was a wealthy businessman with very considerable organisational flair; he it was who set the Model Railway Club on its feet, being its Chairman and then President for some thirty years. He was also Chairman of Bassett-Lowke, as well as being a Director of the Leeds Model Co., which he heavily subsidised. He was truly one of the pioneers of the hobby, but because of his retiring nature one tended to hear little of him. He was also a Director of Winteringham's, the factory engineering side of Bassett-Lowke, and Leslie Huckle, then an apprentice at Winteringham's, was the builder of many of the Pantry Dockyard Railway's locomotives. Among G.P. Keen's models were examples by the young Stanley Beeson. Keen spoke French fluently, spent much time on business on the continent, and included a great number of continental prototypes in his model collection, including some rather remarkable sleeping cars. These were built by a Frenchman with a name whose spelling I can only guess at, but it sounds like Mascel Rossi.

M. Rossi received a contract for a number of sleeping cars, the first of which caused Geoffrey Keen some amusement, for not only was it beautifully detailed inside and out, but was populated by a series of delectable young ladies in various states of undress. No prude was Keen, but he did give instructions that "a joke was a joke, but don't bother to fit any more of these nubile young nymphs into the decor of the rest of the set!" Apparently, M. Rossi had other ideas; for him a Wagons-Lits was not a Wagons-Lits unless it resembled something between the dressing room of the Folies Bergère and a girlie magazine. Certainly, the whole thing is very cleverly and tastefully executed; but the trouble is that one's attention is apt to be distracted from the very fine detailed finish of the coaches by their inhabitants! Mrs Keen told me that Geoffrey used to remark that he seemed to be involved in super-detailed models in more ways than one. All these sleeping cars, after Keen's death, were marshalled decorously with the windows facing the wall of the room, and to see them one had to crawl under the baseboard to reach the other side – I strained my back quite badly! It was noticeable that when one looked out of the windows of the railway room in this house, perched up on the cliffs above Hythe, one looked straight into Boulogne Harbour.

It is not perhaps altogether surprising, although remarkable, how, as I travelled about the country visiting all these people, I would encounter links in the most unexpected places. Whilst making a programme on the very fine pre-grouping Great Northern railway of Ian King, I found that he had been a close friend for many years of Geoff Bigmore. Bigmore, again, with Eagles, and so on – showing clearly how the influence of one gifted man inspired others.

It has been remarked before that, unlike so many of the hobbies pursued by men, railway modelling seems so free from the jealousies and rivalries of other pastimes. Consider the tales of espionage and sabotage among competitors at floral and agricultural shows, and compare that with the spirit of tolerance and helpfulness which seems to pervade the model railway scene – and nowhere more so than in Gauge 0.

To all intents and purposes Crewchester is now virtually complete and, with Ken Payne, I could describe it as 'The Last Great Project', although, like John Hart, I shall continue to try to 'improve the breed'. The Guild slide/cassette collection should have been started twenty-five years ago, for even as I write, with 130 programmes available on loan to Guild members, I have barely scratched the surface of this hobby. Guild membership is growing fast, with its concomitant problems in management, and doubtless as the years go by, better and better model railways will appear. But, looking back on the decade of the 1980s, they have been perhaps some of the best years of my life – something they never tell you when you are young! Old age, they tell us, is a time of increasing ill-health and decreasing capabilities, but it need not be. Looking back over those ten years and all the people I have met, all the homes I have stayed in, and the model railways I have seen, I sometimes wonder, were the terrible choice to be thrust upon me, which of all those model layouts I would choose if I were told only one may be retained.

Just as every parent has a favourite child, even though loving them all, I have my own favourite. Not because it was necessarily the best, or because it has the finest models, or the best scenery, or any other tangible superiority over all others, but merely because, for me, it contained the qualities which appealed to me personally; so much so that when I sit by that railway in full session, I am really transported back to the days of steam in a way that no other model railway has ever quite equalled.

For me, this railway is Ken Longbottom's 'Diggle and Westport', a line which has not, so far, been discussed. To those who have seen it, there is nothing I can write which will add significantly to what they already know. For those who have never seen it, let me try to offer a picture of what to me constitutes the ideal model railway.

Based upon LNWR practice and locale, this extensive system runs round a very large garden, passing through four buildings on the way, each of which houses a block-post. Because the Wirral is one of the wettest parts of Britain, the outside sections are protected by weather-proof casings, but in the event of fine weather these covers may be removed. The stations, Diggle, Hale Barns and Westport (with one or two other subsidiary stations), are all based upon recognisable LNWR and North Staffordshire railway architecture, and are detailed down to the smallest item. The block posts are sufficiently far apart to ensure that when a tapper-key is pressed it is impossible to hear the bell the other end, thereby preserving the illusion of great distance. Ken himself is an authority on signalling and is responsible for all the signals on the railway, with full interlocking. No train may move unless the correct signal is pulled off (an admittedly debatable practice, but it does ensure that signals which were installed with considerable trouble and effort are not ignored). Scale length trains have ample room in scale length stations; none of your five-coach maximum here! Full timetable working is observed, and it requires at least eight experienced operators to run a full session – and these operators do come, from near and far. Friday evening will see a four-hour session from 8pm to midnight, followed by refreshments and a further meeting, film-show, or just a get-together of enthusiasts. The nearest I have ever seen to Diggle and Westport was Vic Martin's amazing setup on the Isle of Sheppey, but here, unlike there, we have near to fine-scale models and track, and a sequence of stations instead of just the one 80ft visible section of track.

The Pendeford Line of Maurice Nagington also comes very close to Diggle and Westport in both scale and *modus operandi*, but then I have seen that line only once, when I photographed it for the Guild; never in full session. But Diggle and Westport has, for me, achieved the near-impossible, and every one of those stations is an exercise in pure postalgia: a return to those far-off days when I travelled the British Isles by steam train.

Hale Barns station takes me back to the days when I did much travelling; and when the main lights are extinguished in that shed, the model comes to life in a very moving way. The soft light coming from the waiting rooms and station lamps, the coloured dots of light from the semaphore signals, the street lamps reflected in the shop windows – shops run by old-established families and not gaunt warehouses where one can buy everything from bread to bath mats! Chemists sold drugs and medicines, stationers sold stationery, greengrocers fruit and vegetables, sweet-shops sold confectionery. The streets themselves were surfaced by stone setts, the lighting was by gas, and from the dim lighting of Station Road one could see reflected in the low cloud of the night sky the lights of the not-too-distant town centre. Then, round the corner comes the evidence of a railway station, sight, sound and smell all supporting the illusion. Through the door of the booking hall, across the echoing boards of the floor, to the ornate crush-barrier by the ticket office, framing the head-and-shoulders of some other-world being, the thud of the ticket machine, and the descent of the broad staircase with its corrugated treads, flanked by smoke-grimed windows which long ago gave up any attempt to admit light in either direction, and on to the dimly lit platform.

Ken Longbottom has got it all there, down the very last detail, and although I have sat in that shed many times, it never fails in its magic. At one end of the station the tracks dive into a murky tunnel where trains were lost to sight and sound, while at the other end is the magnificent prospect of a network of tracks, including the electrified lines use by the electric multiple units from Diggle (for it is here at Hale Barns where the electric section ends in a bay, with massive hydraulic buffers proclaiming the end of the road). And a great LNWR pattern signal box perched high up above the tracks, in the way such boxes once did, commands clear views of the entire station complex. A handsome gantry of semaphores spans the tracks, with theatre-type route indicators, and, seen

dimly beyond all this, is the tunnel which leads – where? One knows that it *does* lead to Diggle, but as that station is totally unseen or unheard, the illusion of limitless distance is preserved.

Over against the smoke-encrusted wall on a siding stands a row of PMV and other parcels vehicles looking as if they had been there since time itself began, a layer of dust doing nothing to destroy the effect, the ghostly half-light failing to reveal what daylight shows – that we are indeed in a shed, with a roof – all that is lost in darkness. Bells sound from the signal box: 'Call Attention' – an express is offered and accepted and needle peggers tick over to 'Line Clear' – then 'Train in Section' and then – – – silence. Head close to track, as if I was standing on the other end of the platform, I look into the murk and gloom of the tunnel, and a distant rumble is heard.

From some unseen bend in the tracks, the dim outline of a train appears, the rumbling growing to a roar. The metals take on an incandescent glow from the fire in the engine and along the sooty walls of the tunnel one can see the lights reflected from the coaches, until out of the tunnel comes a gleaming red 'Claughton' in full flight, bringing behind it twelve crimson coaches. The combined noise of the train's passing, coupled with the urgent sound of signal bells – acknowledging – announcing – confirming – send the blood racing, and then, a moment later, the train is swallowed up in the tunnel as it makes for Westport. Silence descends upon the room, broken perhaps by the sound of a tea-cup on saucer, a casual length and snatch of conversation in the signal box; relaxation – and preparation for the next movement. Time to wander up to the High Street to see if perhaps there may still be a pie-and-peas shop, or a fish-and-chip shop still open, for it is a long time since dinner, and my train is not due for half an hour.

Mounting the stairs again, and passing through the booking hall, where the single gas lamp plops and splutters, out to the street with its row of shops, all barred and closed for business, the eye is caught by the window of the jeweller, filled wth silver plates of all descriptions, every tiny piece carried out in foil and silver paper. The fascia board with its deeply engraved gold-leaf lettering speaks of another age – maybe the days before the first world war? – and the other, more prosaic shops, greengrocer, newsagent, and the empty shop with its bare window (what human story lies behind that?) all add to this nostalgic microcosm of the days of steam. Away to the left, at the far end of the street, stands the church, its tower silhouetted against the lights of the main part of the town, and the street lamps cast little patches of light on the pavement as one or two lone individuals, probably killing time until their train is due, peer into the shop windows.

There must be other model railways which have the same magic, but it so happens that circumstances have made it possible for me to stay with Ken Longbottom and spend several evenings there, closely observing the scene. Maurice Nagington's railway is very similar in concept, but I have never seen it running; only as a subject for my camera, and the same may be said for Michael Ivor-Jones' vast LD&EC Railway and many others – so where do I stop?

I can admire the efforts of those who, with minimum space available, have wrought miracles of planning to build a model railway in a small area. Not everyone has unlimited space wherein they may run their trains; not everyone even wants to run their trains over vast distances, and for them, the spare bedroom, the garden shed, or even the loft offers the opportunity to produce something of limited scope, yet into which has gone concentrated attention to detail denied to the man who runs a little empire of railway network.

There can be few hobbies which offer such a wealth of choice, such a bewildering vista of possibilities in which to work, nor do I know of a hobby wherein so much mutual tolerance and interest is found. So many of these smaller layouts have impressed me – Frank Roomes with his 'Lutton', Ken Brennan with his 'Rowbarrow Hundred', Robin Lee with 'Gayton Wharf' – and many others far too numerous to mention – have made exciting subjects for my cameras. Moreover, they serve the purpose of their existence – to offer recreation and fulfilment to their owners.

As the owner of a large garden-railway it is understandable that my personal preference is for model railways which offer a sense of distance and space, where trains really do cover considerable distances. Among these are Deryck Featherstone's 'Wingham Branch', Barrie Walls's 'Wallsea Main', David East's garden railway – again the list is too long to include here. There are other railways which appeal strongly by reason of personal knowledge of the terrain they cover. There never was a railway system on the Isle of Skye, but when I see Nigel Goff's narrow-gauge railway with its evocative station names of Kyleakin, Dunvegan, and Portree -- all places I know well – then I see the country through which that line might have gone. 'Kerry Bridge', another superbly atmospheric exhibition layout, depicts Irish narrow gauge in a totally convincing manner. Anyone who has crossed from Stranraer to Larne, and knows the Galloway terminus would feel at home on Michael Mather's Stranraer to Newton Stewart railway. Similarly, anyone who once travelled the Midland and Great Northern system, especially in Norfolk and the Fen country would immediately identify with John Hobden's 'Norfolk Joint Railway'. 'Chewton Mendip' by Bob Harper is an exquisite panorama of Great Western country, while in Gauge One, live steam, exists a breath-taking railway in the grounds of a beautiful country house, run by the West Midlands Group.

Mike Butler, who, inspired by Don Neale, has built a beautiful scenic garden railway in Gauge 0 and radio-controlled is another; but not content with this, he has built out in his garden a signal box – three-quarters full size, in the tappet-room of which lies his nerve-centre, and in the main cabin above is his wife's amenities room.

And there you see my problem; already this is beginning to read like a catalogue – a catalogue with so many important omissions, and with so much remaining untold, but even with the complete list of all the railways I have photographed and all the delightful people I have met, the story of model railways has had its surface barely scratched. I return from each one of these model railways as I return from a concert where some great artiste has played, inspired to do just that little better myself. I shall never aspire to the high standards of Norris, Miller, Maskelyne and the other giants; but when I do return home and sit on a warm summer's day beside Crewchester Junction, controller in hand, looking down through Greystone cutting and awaiting the appearance of a train which is due, then I know beyond all doubt – there is no place quite like one's own back yard.

John Hart's 'King Arthur' *at Ravensmoor on the occasion of its visit, as described in the story of the opening ceremony of Ravensmoor.*

EPILOGUE

The story started in 1916, with this tailpiece being written in 1992 at the age of 75. Developments and improvements to my model railway are taking place all the time, and will continue to do so for as long as I am able. There is no such thing as standing still – there lies stagnation – but only going forward or slipping back, and looking back over the years I have much to regret, and much cause for rejoicing. Lack of careful planning, lost opportunities, and sheer laziness are not matters for self-congratulation, and in fact, were I to be called to account for my accomplishments over the past seventy-odd years I would be hard put to it to point to anything significant in the technical progress of the hobby; rather am I the happy survivor of a bygone age of railway modelling, and content to be so.

The most I would claim is as a communicator. Articles have been published by the score in various model railway publications, but letters between friends, acquaintances, and even perfect strangers must surely be counted in thousands. This compulsive urge to communicate led to the establishment of the Gauge 0 Guild Slide/Cassette scheme, whereby people who have never met, and are unlikely ever to meet, are able to see what 'the other chap' is doing, and thereby gain encouragement and inspiration. This has – over the past decade – been truly a labour of love. It brought me in touch with the very finest model-builders of our time, as well as tentative beginners, and has brought me into contact with all manner of people and every kind of model railway. For such riches in retirement no words can express my heartfelt gratitude.

Crewchester Junction in clockwork days with freight very much in evidence.